Language: Usage and Pr

Contents

Contents continued

Contents continued

Unit 4: Capitalization and Punctuation

Unit 5: Composition

Unit 6: Study Skills

The *Language: Usage and Practice* series meets many needs.

- It is designed for students who require additional practice in the basics of effective writing and speaking.
- It provides focused practice in key grammar, usage, mechanics, and composition areas.
- It helps students gain ownership of essential skills.
- It presents practice exercises in a clear, concise format in a logical sequence.
- It allows for easy and independent use.

The *Language: Usage and Practice* lessons are organized into a series of units arranged in a logical sequence.

- vocabulary
- sentences
- grammar and usage
- mechanics of capitalization and punctuation
- composition skills

The *Language: Usage and Practice* lessons are carefully formatted for student comfort.

- Systematic, focused attention is given to just one carefully selected skill at a time.
- Rules are clearly stated at the beginning of each lesson and are illustrated with examples.
- Key terms are introduced in bold type.
- Meaningful practice exercises reinforce the skill.
- Each lesson is clearly labeled, and directions are clear and uncomplicated.

The *Language: Usage and Practice* series stresses the application of language principles in a variety of ways.

- Students are asked to match, circle, or underline elements in a predetermined sentence.
- Students are also asked to use what they have learned in an original sentence or in rewriting a sentence.

Language: Usage and Practice 5, SV 1419027824

The *Language: Usage and Practice* series is designed for independent use.

- ▣ Because the format is logical and consistent and the vocabulary is carefully controlled, students can use *Language: Usage and Practice* with a high degree of independence.
- ▣ Copies of the worksheets can be given to individuals, pairs of students, or small groups for completion.
- ▣ Worksheets can be used in the language arts center.
- ▣ Worksheets can be given as homework for reviewing and reinforcing skills.

The *Language: Usage and Practice* series provides writing instruction.

- ▣ The process approach to teaching writing provides success for most students.
- ▣ *Language: Usage and Practice* provides direct support for the teaching of composition and significantly enhances those strategies and techniques commonly associated with the process-writing approach.
- ▣ Each book includes a composition unit that provides substantial work with composition skills, such as writing topic sentences, selecting supporting details, taking notes, writing reports, and revising and proofreading.
- ▣ Also included in the composition unit is practice with various prewriting activities, such as clustering and brainstorming, which play an important part in process writing.
- ▣ The composition lessons are presented in the same rule-plus-practice format as in the other units.

The *Language: Usage and Practice* series includes additional features.

- ▣ **Unit Tests**   Use the unit tests to check student progress and prepare students for standardized tests.
- ▣ **Sequential Support**   The content of each unit is repeated and expanded in subsequent levels as highlighted in the skills correlation chart on pages 5 and 6.
- ▣ **Assessment**   Use the Assessment on pages 7–10 to determine the skills your students need to practice.
- ▣ **Language Terms**   Provide each student with a copy of the list of language terms on page 120 to keep for reference throughout the year.
- ▣ **Small-Group Activities**   Use the worksheets as small-group activities to give students the opportunity to work cooperatively.

The *Language: Usage and Practice* series is a powerful tool!

**The activities use a variety of strategies to maintain student interest.
Watch your students' language improve as skills are
applied in structured, relevant practice!**

Language: Usage and Practice 5, SV 1419027824

Skills Correlation

	1	2	3	4	5	6	7	8	High School
Vocabulary									
Rhyming Words	■	■							
Synonyms and Antonyms	■	■	■	■	■	■	■	■	■
Homonyms	■	■	■	■	■	■	■	■	■
Multiple Meanings/Homographs	■	■	■	■	■	■	■	■	■
Prefixes and Suffixes		■	■	■	■	■	■	■	■
Compound Words		■	■	■	■	■	■	■	■
Contractions		■	■	■	■	■	■	■	■
Idioms						■	■	■	■
Connotation/Denotation					■	■	■	■	
Sentences									
Word Order in Sentences	■	■		■					
Recognizing Sentences and Sentence Types	■	■	■	■	■	■	■	■	■
Subjects and Predicates	■	■	■	■	■	■	■	■	■
Compound/Complex Sentences			■	■	■	■	■	■	■
Sentence Combining		■	■	■	■	■	■	■	■
Run-on Sentences			■	■	■	■	■	■	■
Independent and Subordinate Clauses							■	■	■
Compound Subjects and Predicates	■			■		■	■	■	■
Direct and Indirect Objects					■		■	■	■
Inverted Word Order						■	■	■	■
Grammar and Usage									
Common and Proper Nouns	■	■	■	■	■	■	■	■	■
Singular and Plural Nouns	■	■	■	■	■	■	■	■	■
Possessive Nouns			■	■	■	■	■	■	■
Appositives						■	■	■	
Verbs and Verb Tense	■	■	■	■	■	■	■	■	■
Regular/Irregular Verbs	■	■	■	■	■	■	■	■	■
Subject/Verb Agreement	■	■	■	■	■	■	■	■	■
Verb Phrases						■	■	■	■
Transitive and Intransitive Verbs							■	■	
Verbals: Gerunds, Participles, and Infinitives							■	■	■
Active and Passive Voice							■	■	
Mood								■	
Pronouns	■	■	■	■	■	■	■	■	■
Antecedents					■		■	■	■
Articles	■	■	■		■	■			
Adjectives	■	■	■	■	■	■	■	■	■
Correct Word Usage (e.g., may/can, sit/set)	■		■	■	■	■	■	■	■
Adverbs			■	■	■	■	■	■	■
Prepositions					■	■	■	■	■
Prepositional Phrases					■	■	■	■	■
Conjunctions					■	■	■	■	■
Interjections					■	■			
Double Negatives							■	■	■
Capitalization and Punctuation									
Capitalization: First Word in Sentence	■	■	■	■	■	■	■	■	■
Capitalization: Proper Nouns	■	■	■	■	■	■	■	■	■
Capitalization: in Letters			■	■	■	■	■	■	■
Capitalization: Abbreviations and Titles		■	■	■	■	■	■	■	■
Capitalization: Proper Adjectives					■	■	■	■	■

Skills Correlation

Language: Usage and Practice 5, SV 1419027824

	1	2	3	4	5	6	7	8	High School
Capitalization and Punctuation (cont'd)									
End Punctuation	■	■	■	■	■	■	■	■	■
Commas		■	■	■	■	■	■	■	■
Apostrophes in Contractions		■	■	■	■	■	■	■	■
Apostrophes in Possessives			■	■	■	■	■	■	■
Quotation Marks			■	■	■	■	■	■	■
Colons/Semicolons					■	■	■	■	■
Hyphens						■	■	■	■
Composition									
Expanding Sentences				■		■	■	■	■
Paragraphs: Topic Sentence (main idea)		■	■	■	■	■	■	■	■
Paragraphs: Supporting Details		■	■	■	■	■	■	■	■
Order in Paragraphs			■	■	■	■	■		■
Writing Process:									
Audience				■	■	■	■	■	
Topic			■	■	■	■	■	■	
Outlining				■		■	■	■	
Clustering/Brainstorming					■		■	■	
Note Taking						■			
Revising/Proofreading					■	■	■	■	
Types of Writing:									
Poem	■								
Letter	■	■	■			■			
"How-to" Paragraph				■					
Invitation				■					
Telephone Message				■					
Conversation					■				
Narrative Paragraph					■				
Comparing and Contrasting						■			
Descriptive Paragraph						■			
Report							■		
Interview								■	
Persuasive Composition									■
Readiness/Study Skills									
Grouping	■		■						
Letters of Alphabet	■								
Listening	■	■							
Making Comparisons	■	■							
Organizing Information			■	■					
Following Directions	■	■	■	■	■				
Alphabetical Order	■	■	■	■	■				
Using a Dictionary:									
Definitions			■	■			■	■	■
Guide Words/Entry Words			■	■	■	■	■	■	■
Syllables and Pronunciation						■	■	■	■
Multiple Meanings			■	■			■	■	■
Word Origins							■	■	■
Parts of a Book			■					■	
Using the Library							■	■	■
Using Encyclopedias					■	■	■	■	■
Using Reference Books							■	■	■
Using the *Readers' Guide*								■	■
Using Tables, Charts, Graphs, and Diagrams								■	
Choosing Appropriate Sources							■	■	■

Skills Correlation
Language: Usage and Practice 5, SV 1419027824

Name _____ Date _____

Assessment

�֍ **Write S before each pair of synonyms, A before each pair of antonyms, and H before each pair of homonyms.**

_____ 1. river, stream

_____ 2. new, knew

_____ 3. ugly, pretty

_____ 4. threw, through

�֍ **Write the homograph for the pair of meanings.**

_____ 5. **a.** a formal dance   **b.** a round object

✷ **Write P before each word with a prefix, S before each word with a suffix, and C before each compound word.**

_____ 6. shoelace

_____ 7. mistrust

_____ 8. firmness

_____ 9. downstairs

✷ **Write the words that make up each contraction.**

_____ 10. won't

_____ 11. he'll

✷ **Write D before the declarative sentence, IM before the imperative sentence, E before the exclamatory sentence, and IN before the interrogative sentence. Then circle the simple subject and underline the simple predicate in each sentence.**

_____ 12. Happy days are here again!

_____ 13. What do you mean by that?

_____ 14. I really like my life right now.

_____ 15. You should take it one day at a time.

✷ **Write CS before the sentence with a compound subject. Write CP before the sentence with a compound predicate.**

_____ 16. Apples and oranges are my favorite fruits.

_____ 17. The wind howled and shrieked.

✷ **Write CS before the compound sentence. Write RO before the run-on sentence.**

_____ 18. Since it was raining, we went inside, we sat and watched it rain.

_____ 19. It didn't stop raining, so we played card games.

✷ **Underline the common nouns, and circle the proper nouns in the sentence.**

20. Jon told Rachel that her dog had been found in the park.

7

Name _____ Date _____

✸ **Write the correct possessive noun to complete the second sentence.**

21. The headlight of our car burned out. Our _____ headlight burned out.

✸ **Write A if the underlined verb is an action verb, L if it is a linking verb, or H if it is a helping verb.**

_____ 22. We <u>were</u> waiting our turn.

_____ 23. It <u>felt</u> good to be there.

_____ 24. We <u>helped</u> as often as possible.

✸ **Write past, present, or future to show the tense of each underlined verb.**

_____ 25. Someone <u>will come</u> soon.

_____ 26. They <u>left</u> an hour later.

_____ 27. She <u>is walking</u> with her children.

✸ **Circle the correct verb in each sentence.**

28. (Do, Did) you (see, saw) what happened?

29. He (drink, drank) the water and then (broke, break) the glass.

30. She has (wrote, written) a hit song and has (sang, sung) it on TV.

31. We (eaten, ate) a big meal and (begun, began) to get sleepy.

✸ **Write SP before the sentence that has a subject pronoun, OP before the sentence that has an object pronoun, and PP before the sentence that has a possessive pronoun.**

_____ 32. My grandparents were successful farmers.

_____ 33. They always lived out in the country.

_____ 34. Mother told me about the farm.

✸ **On the line before each sentence, write adjective or adverb to describe the underlined word.**

_____ 35. Exercise is part of my <u>daily</u> activities.

_____ 36. I run <u>often</u>.

✸ **In the sentence below, underline each prepositional phrase and circle each preposition.**

37. An oil spot was on the floor of the garage.

Assessment
Language: Usage and Practice 5, SV 1419027824

Name _____ Date _____

❀ Circle the correct word in parentheses to complete each sentence.

38. (Teach, Learn) me how to bake.

39. We will have a (well, good) time together.

40. Get the eggs and (sit, set) them on the counter.

41. Now (sit, set) on the stool.

42. You (can, may) separate the eggs.

❀ In the letter below, underline letters that should be capitalized and add punctuation where needed.

487 e deer run

sacramento ca 94099

feb 27 2007

dear luke

whats it like living in california ____ i cant even imagine it ____ the postcards you sent were fantastic ____ it will be fun to come and visit ____ im worried about earthquakes, though ____

take care of yourself ____

your friend

paul

❀ Expand the meaning of the sentence base below.

43. Students created. _____

❀ Write a topic sentence and two sentences with descriptive supporting details on the topic of pollution.

44. _____

45. _____

46. _____

❀ Number the following directions in order.

_____ 47. Turn on the dishwasher.

_____ 48. Load dirty dishes in the machine.

_____ 49. Put soap in the dispenser.

Assessment
Language: Usage and Practice 5, SV 1419027824

Name _____ Date _____

 Read the guide words. Then write the words from the box that would be found on the same page, placing a hyphen between syllables.

slop / sneer

50. _____

51. _____

52. _____

sliding	silver
slumber	smattering
snuggle	sluggish

 Use the sample encyclopedia entry to answer the questions.

LOCK   Locks are sets of gates that help ships move through canals. Each lock is on a different level, and two sets of gates make up each lock. The locks are similar to stairs. A ship moves into a lock, and the gates in front of and behind the ship close. Water is then pumped into or let out of the enclosed lock. This raises or lowers the ship to the level of the next lock. *See also* CANAL.

53. What is the article about? _____

54. What do locks do? _____

55. How many sets of gates does a lock have? _____

56. What are locks compared to in the article? _____

57. What is the cross-reference? _____

 The example below shows how the volumes of a small encyclopedia are marked. Circle the word you would look under to find an article on each of the following subjects. Then write the number of the volume in which you would find each article.

A–C	D–F	G–H	I–L	M–N	O–R	S–T	U–W	X–Z
1	2	3	4	5	6	7	8	9

_____ **58.** the history of mining

_____ **59.** Mark Twain

_____ **60.** the Nile River

_____ **61.** plant life of the tundra

_____ **62.** the capital of Sweden

_____ **63.** Great Danes

_____ **64.** Japanese gardens

_____ **65.** how volcanoes erupt

Name _____   Date _____

Synonyms

> • A **synonym** is a word that has the same or nearly the same
> meaning as one or more other words.
>   EXAMPLES: help—aid—assist   cold—chilly—wintry

 **Write one synonym for each word below. Write another synonym
in a short phrase. Underline the synonym in the phrase.**

1. small   _____little_____   _____<u>tiny</u> bug_____

2. enormous   _____   _____

3. vehicle   _____   _____

4. select   _____   _____

5. complete   _____   _____

6. river   _____   _____

7. permit   _____   _____

8. speedy   _____   _____

 For each word in parentheses, write a synonym on the line.

9. Many trees in an old forest are (high) _____.

10. Underneath them grow (lower) _____ trees and plants.

11. As the (aged) _____ trees die, they make room for others.

12. Sometimes fires will (destroy) _____ the entire forest.

13. Then from the (charred) _____ earth sprout new plants.

14. They all begin their (stretch) _____ for the sky again.

 **Write three sentences about the forest. In each sentence, use a
synonym for one of the words below. Underline the synonym.**

begin	lofty	soil

15. _____

16. _____

17. _____

Unit 1: Vocabulary
Language: Usage and Practice 5, SV 1419027824

Name _____ Date _____

Antonyms

> • An **antonym** is a word that has the opposite meaning of another word.
> EXAMPLES: hot—cold   tall—short

✳ **Write an antonym for the underlined word in each phrase below.**

1. dark blue _____
2. busy worker _____
3. up the hill _____
4. noisy play _____
5. north wind _____
6. buy a car _____
7. time of day _____
8. bitter taste _____
9. come now _____
10. good dog _____
11. small bird _____
12. rough road _____
13. black coat _____
14. above the neck _____

15. frowning face _____
16. under the bridge _____
17. pretty color _____
18. cold water _____
19. feeling strong _____
20. wide belt _____
21. unhappy face _____
22. east side _____
23. cool breeze _____
24. stop the car _____
25. heavy jacket _____
26. long story _____
27. give a gift _____
28. difficult task _____

✳ **For each word in parentheses, write an antonym on the line.**

We were very (**29.** sad) _____ to be on vacation. It was the

(**30.** last) _____ time we had been able to (**31.** stay) _____

in a long time, and this one would be really (**32.** boring) _____.

We rented a cabin in the (**33.** low) _____ mountains of Colorado.

We were hoping for (**34.** hot) _____ and snowy weather so we

could ski. The (**35.** last) _____ thing we did when we got to

the cabin was (**36.** pack) _____ our clothes. Then we hiked

around (**37.** inside) _____. We liked being in such a

(**38.** terrible) _____ place.

Name _____ Date _____

Homonyms

> • **Homonyms** are words that are pronounced alike but are spelled
> differently and have different meanings.
>   EXAMPLES: I'll—aisle   two—too—to

 **Write a short phrase that includes a homonym for each word
below. Circle each homonym.**

1. haul _____

2. road _____

3. sum _____

4. way _____

5. new _____

6. meat _____

> • <u>Two</u> is a number.
> • <u>Too</u> means "also," "besides," or "more than enough."
> • <u>To</u> means "toward." It is also used with such words as <u>be</u>, <u>sing</u>,
>   <u>play</u>, and other action words.

 **Write <u>two</u>, <u>too</u>, or <u>to</u> on the line to complete each sentence
correctly.**

7. Ben was _____ frightened _____ utter a word.

8. He had heard the strange sound _____ times.

9. He went _____ his room upstairs, _____ steps at a time. But he heard it there,

   _____.

10. He decided _____ call his friend who lived _____ blocks away. It seemed the

   only thing _____ do!

> • <u>Their</u> means "belonging to them."
> • <u>There</u> means "in that place."
> • <u>They're</u> is a contraction of the words <u>they are</u>.

 Underline the correct word in parentheses.

11. They are over (their, there, they're) standing in (their, there, they're) yard.

12. (Their, There, They're) waiting to go visit (their, there, they're) friends.

13. (Their, There, They're) going to leave for (their, there, they're) vacation.

Name _____   Date _____

Troublesome Words

- Use <u>too</u> when you mean "very" or "also." Use <u>to</u> when you mean "in the direction of." Use <u>two</u> when you mean the numeral 2.
- Use <u>it's</u> when you mean "it is." Use <u>its</u> when you mean "belonging to it."
- Use <u>their</u> when you mean "belonging to them." Use <u>there</u> when you mean "in that place." Use <u>they're</u> when you mean "they are."
- Use <u>your</u> when you mean "belonging to you." Use <u>you're</u> when you mean "you are."
- The word <u>good</u> is an adjective. Use <u>good</u> to describe a noun.
- Use <u>well</u> as an adjective when you mean "healthy." Use <u>well</u> as an adverb when you tell how something is done.

 Circle the word in parentheses that correctly completes each sentence.

1. We went (to, too, two) the aquarium.

2. Len stayed home because he did not feel (good, well).

3. (Its, It's) a great place to visit.

4. You forgot to bring (you're, your) lunch.

5. (To, Too, Two) beluga whales were (there, their, they're).

6. One whale had a cute spot on (its, it's) face.

7. (You're, Your) the first person I told about our trip.

8. I wish you had been able to come, (to, too, two).

9. It was a (good, well) idea to take the trip.

10. (There, Their, They're) very happy to have students visit them.

11. The fish and other sea animals are taken care of (good, well).

12. We saw the sea otters eat (there, their, they're) meal.

13. I think (its, it's) worthwhile to go again.

14. Did you see the (to, too, two) walruses?

15. (There, Their, They're) sea lions, not walruses.

16. Look at those (to, too, two) dolphins over (there, their, they're).

Language: Usage and Practice 5, SV 1419027824

Name _____ Date _____

Homographs

> • **Homographs** are words that are spelled the same but have different meanings. They may also be pronounced differently.
>   EXAMPLE: <u>Desert</u> means "a barren, dry place," and <u>desert</u> also means "to abandon."

 Read each sentence and the two meanings for the underlined word. Circle the meaning that tells how the word is used in the sentence.

1. The soldiers' <u>arms</u> were old and rusty.

   a. parts of the body   **b.** weapons for war

2. Several had made <u>bats</u> from fallen tree limbs.

   a. flying mammals   **b.** rounded wooden clubs

3. The <u>long</u> war had made them all tired.

   a. extending over a considerable time   **b.** to wish for

4. They were all ready to go <u>back</u> home.

   a. part of the body   **b.** to a place from which a person came

5. They hoped someone would <u>lead</u> them to safety.

   a. soft, gray metal   **b.** to show the way

 Write the homograph for each pair of meanings below. The first letter of each word is given for you.

6. **a.** sound made with fingers   **b.** a metal fastener   s_____

7. **a.** lame walk or step   **b.** not stiff   l_____

8. **a.** use oars to move a boat   **b.** a noisy fight   r_____

9. **a.** a tree covering   **b.** the sound a dog makes   b_____

10. **a.** to press flat   **b.** a yellow vegetable   s_____

Write pairs of sentences that show two different meanings for each homograph below. Use a dictionary if necessary.

11. school _____

   _____

12. pupil _____

   _____

Unit 1: Vocabulary
Language: Usage and Practice 5, SV 1419027824

Name _____ Date _____

Prefixes and Suffixes

- A **prefix** or a **suffix** added to a base word changes the meaning of the word.
    - EXAMPLE: <u>re</u> meaning "again" + the base word <u>do</u> = <u>redo</u> meaning "to do again"
- Re means "again," <u>pre</u> means "before," <u>mis</u> means "wrongly" or "not," <u>able</u> means "that can be," <u>less</u> means "without," <u>ness</u> means "state of being."

 Write the word formed by each combination. Then write the definition of the new word.

1. kind + ness = _____

2. pre + date = _____

3. help + less = _____

4. re + made = _____

 Read each sentence. Use one of the prefixes or suffixes and the base word in parentheses to form a new word. Write the new word on the line.

mis	ful	pre	less	re	ness

5. Teresa _____ her vacations by viewing the photographs she took.
   (lives)

6. She spends _____ hours enjoying the mountain scenery.
   (end)

7. Her favorite shot shows a mountain sunset just before

   _____ settled over their campsite.
   (dark)

8. Jon didn't see Perry's look of fright when a bear made a

   _____ raid on the garbage can.
   (dawn)

9. Jon had _____ the camera directions in dim light.
   (read)

10. He did, however, get a shot of the bear's _____ cubs.
    (delight)

Language: Usage and Practice 5, SV 1419027824

Name _____   Date _____

Contractions

> • A **contraction** is a word formed by joining two other words.
> • An **apostrophe (')** shows where a letter or letters have been left out.
>   EXAMPLES: it is = it's   we will = we'll

 Write the contraction formed by the words.

1. who + is = _____
2. could + not = _____
3. they + have = _____
4. I + will = _____
5. does + not = _____
6. should + have = _____

7. you + would = _____
8. I + have = _____
9. that + is = _____
10. did + not = _____
11. let + us = _____
12. they + are = _____

 Use the contractions below to complete each sentence. Write the contractions on the lines.

| can't | couldn't | he'll | I'm | it's | I've |
| She's | wasn't | What'll | What's | Where's | Let's |

13. It _____ quite show time.

14. Diego called out, "_____ Pearl?"

15. "What?" shouted Sara. "_____ not here yet?"

16. "No, and _____ looked everywhere."

17. "The show _____ go on without the star," Sara wailed.

18. Sara added, "_____ we do?"

19. "_____ ask Justin," Diego suggested.

20. "Yes," said Sara, "_____ know what to do."

21. Just then a voice called, "_____ all the excitement?"

22. "Pearl, _____ you!" Sara and Diego exclaimed.

23. "Yes," said Pearl, "I know _____ late."

24. Pearl added, "I _____ find my costume!"

Unit 1: Vocabulary
Language: Usage and Practice 5, SV 1419027824

Name _____ Date _____

Compound Words

> • Compound words may be two words written as one, two words joined by a hyphen, or two separate words.
> EXAMPLES: sunlight   ho-hum   easy chair

 Draw a line between the two words that form each compound word below.

1. high/way
2. old-time
3. full moon
4. snowflake
5. air conditioner

6. fire drill
7. barefoot
8. babysitter
9. splashdown
10. sweatshirt

11. highrise
12. earthquake
13. half-mast
14. bulldog
15. skateboard

 Use two of the words below to form a compound word that will complete each numbered sentence. Write the word on the line.

after   back   come   hard   hood   neighbor   noon   out   ware   yard

16. Jan and I bought a hammer and nails at a _____ store.

17. Part of the fence in our _____ was broken.

18. It took most of the _____ to repair the fence.

19. We were proud of the _____.

20. Our fence was the finest in the _____.

 Use the second word part of each compound word to make the next compound word. Write the new word.

21. **clubhouse** — a building used by a club

_____houseboat_____ — a boat that people can live in

_____boathouse_____ — a house for storing boats

22. **teacup** — a cup for drinking tea

_____ — a cake the size of a cup

_____ — a circular walking game in which players may win a cake

Language: Usage and Practice 5, SV 1419027824

Name _____ Date _____

Negatives

> • A <u>negative</u> is a word that means "no" or "not."
> • The words <u>never</u>, <u>no</u>, <u>nobody</u>, <u>none</u>, <u>not</u>, <u>nothing</u>, and <u>nowhere</u> are negatives.
> • The negative word <u>not</u> is often used in contractions.
> • Do not use two negatives in the same sentence.
> > EXAMPLES:
> > Erika had **never** worked in a big store before.
> > **Nobody** there knew her.
> > She **didn't** know at first what she should do.

 Complete each sentence by choosing the correct word in parentheses. Avoid using two negatives in the same sentence.

1. Most people _____ never get a snakebite.
   (will, won't)

2. If you do get bitten, don't go into _____ panic.
   (a, no)

3. Remember that not all snakes _____ poisonous.
   (are, aren't)

4. It's best not to do _____ that will speed the spread of the poison.
   (anything, nothing)

5. Didn't _____ in our group ever study this before?
   (anybody, nobody)

6. If you must go for help, don't _____ run.
   (ever, never)

7. When in snake country, don't take _____ chances.
   (any, no)

Each sentence contains a double negative. Cut or replace at least one of the negatives. Write the sentence correctly.

8. There aren't no more than four kinds of poisonous snakes in North America.

   _____

   _____

9. It won't do no good to try to run away from a rattlesnake.

   _____

10. Don't never tease a snake that might bite you.

   _____

Unit 1: Vocabulary
Language: Usage and Practice 5, SV 1419027824

Avoiding Wordy Language

- Good writers say what they mean in as few words as possible.
- When you revise, cross out words that don't add to the meaning.
  EXAMPLE:
  Marci was putting on her clothes and getting ready for Chet's party. (wordy)
  Marci was dressing for Chet's party. (better)

 Rewrite each sentence. Replace the words in parentheses with fewer words.

1. Our family was (putting clothes and other items in) suitcases.

   _____

2. Everyone was looking forward to (the vacation that we take every year).

   _____

3. When all the suitcases were packed, Mom (put all the suitcases in) the trunk.

   _____

4. We (pulled out of the driveway) at noon on Saturday.

   _____

5. We (made our way through the streets) to the freeway.

   _____

6. We (ended up stopping every little while) because my little brother was (not feeling very well).

   _____

7. The first day of travel seemed (to go pretty well), though.

   _____

8. The second day we (stopped off and went to see the sights of) historical places.

   _____

9. Everyone (really had a good time on) the rest of the trip, too.

   _____

10. (Each one of our neighbors) welcomed us back.

   _____

Language: Usage and Practice 5, SV 1419027824

Name _____   Date _____

Using Sensory Images

> • Good writers use **sensory words** that appeal to some or all of the five senses.
>   EXAMPLE:
>   **Cold**, **white** snow blanketed the **green pine** trees in the **quiet** valley.

 Read each sentence. On the line, write each underlined word and tell the sense or senses to which it most appeals as it is used in the sentence.

1. The young swimmer was wearing a <u>blue</u> suit.

   _____

2. She dove cleanly into the <u>cool</u> water.

   _____

3. The judges wrote the scores in <u>large</u> black letters.

   _____

4. The audience let out a <u>loud</u> cheer.

   _____

5. She had been practicing so long that her hair had the odor of <u>chlorine</u>.

   _____

6. One tile on the practice pool was rough and <u>jagged</u>.

   _____

7. The <u>rough</u> edge had cut her foot, and she had yelled, "Ouch!"

   _____

8. Her coach had put a <u>soft</u> bandage on it, and it was fine now.

   _____

9. The sweatshirt she put on was <u>warm</u> and soft.

   _____

10. After practice, she had a <u>delicious</u> sandwich.

   _____

Unit 1: Vocabulary
Language: Usage and Practice 5, SV 1419027824

Name _____   Date _____

Denotation and Connotation

- The **denotation** of a word is its exact meaning as stated in a dictionary. Denotations use **literal language**.
- The **connotation** of a word is a second, suggested meaning of a word. This added meaning often suggests something positive or negative. Connotations use **figurative language**.

  EXAMPLES:
  Skinny suggests "too thin." Skinny has a negative connotation.
  Slender suggests "attractively thin." Slender has a positive connotation.

- Some words are **neutral**. They do not suggest either good or bad meanings. For example, hat, seventeen, and yearly are neutral words.

 Circle the word in parentheses that has the more positive connotation.

1. Our trip to the amusement park was (good, wonderful).

2. (Brave, Foolhardy) people rode on the roller coaster.

3. We saw (fascinating, weird) animals in the animal house.

4. Some of the monkeys made (hilarious, goofy) faces.

5. Everyone's face wore a (smile, smirk) on the way home.

 Circle the word in parentheses that has the more negative connotation.

6. We bought (cheap, inexpensive) souvenirs at the park.

7. I ate a (soggy, moist) sandwich.

8. Mike (nagged, reminded) us to go to the fun house.

9. He was very (determined, stubborn) about going.

10. The fun house was (comical, silly).

Answer the following questions.

11. Which is more serious, a problem or a disaster?

_____

12. Which is worth more, something old or something antique?

_____

Unit 1: Vocabulary
Language: Usage and Practice 5, SV 1419027824

Using Figurative Language

- Writers often use **figurative language** to compare unlike things. Figurative language uses figures of speech such as **similes**, **metaphors**, and **personification**. Figurative language gives a meaning that is not exactly that of the words used.
- When <u>like</u> or <u>as</u> is used to compare two things, the comparison is called a simile. A metaphor makes a comparison by speaking of one thing as if it were another.
- Sometimes a writer will give human characteristics to nonhuman things. Objects, ideas, places, or animals may be given human qualities. They may perform human actions. This kind of language is called personification.

  EXAMPLES:
  His feet smelled <u>like</u> **dead fish**. (simile)
  Paul Bunyan was <u>as</u> big <u>as</u> a **tree**. (simile)
  The deep **lake** was a **golden mirror** reflecting the setting sun. (metaphor)
  The old tree **moaned with pain** in the cold wind. (personification)

 The sentences below include figurative language. Rewrite each sentence. Express the same idea without using figurative language.

1. I was as jumpy as a cat in a roomful of rocking chairs.

   _____

2. As I looked out over the audience, my heart was a brick in my chest.

   _____

3. I touched the piano keys, and my fingers were like fence posts.

   _____

4. Luckily for me, the performance was as smooth as silk.

   _____

5. The last notes whispered, "You did just fine!"

   _____

 Complete each sentence below by using figurative language.

6. The deserted old house was as dark as _____

7. When I opened the squeaky front door, it creaked _____

Name _____   Date _____

Unit 1 Test

Decide whether the underlined words in each sentence are synonyms, antonyms, homonyms, or homographs. Darken the circle by your answer.

1. My aunt gave me an ant farm for my birthday.
   Ⓐ synonyms   Ⓑ antonyms   Ⓒ homonyms   Ⓓ homographs

2. The tree grew taller and increased in size.
   Ⓐ synonyms   Ⓑ antonyms   Ⓒ homonyms   Ⓓ homographs

3. Lara seemed happy, but inside she was unhappy.
   Ⓐ synonyms   Ⓑ antonyms   Ⓒ homonyms   Ⓓ homographs

4. Did the knight travel by day or by night?
   Ⓐ synonyms   Ⓑ antonyms   Ⓒ homonyms   Ⓓ homographs

5. John left the room and turned left down the hall.
   Ⓐ synonyms   Ⓑ antonyms   Ⓒ homonyms   Ⓓ homographs

6. I traded the dull movie for an exciting book.
   Ⓐ synonyms   Ⓑ antonyms   Ⓒ homonyms   Ⓓ homographs

7. She soon saw that the blade of the saw was bent.
   Ⓐ synonyms   Ⓑ antonyms   Ⓒ homonyms   Ⓓ homographs

8. He heard her shout and then give a yell to call for help.
   Ⓐ synonyms   Ⓑ antonyms   Ⓒ homonyms   Ⓓ homographs

Add a prefix or suffix to the underlined word to make a new word that makes sense in the sentence. Darken the circle by your choice.

9. Traci was able to pay Lionel the money she borrowed.
   Ⓐ mis   Ⓒ ity
   Ⓑ re   Ⓓ less

10. We had a delight vacation.
    Ⓐ er   Ⓒ ful
    Ⓑ pre   Ⓓ ment

11. I like to spend end hours reading.
    Ⓐ er   Ⓒ less
    Ⓑ ity   Ⓓ un

12. How did Janet act to the news?
    Ⓐ er   Ⓒ pro
    Ⓑ re   Ⓓ ment

13. Dark settled over the campsite.
    Ⓐ er   Ⓒ al
    Ⓑ bi   Ⓓ ness

14. We can't read the directions!
    Ⓐ bi   Ⓒ mis
    Ⓑ pro   Ⓓ less

www.harcourtschoolsupply.com
© Harcourt Achieve Inc. All rights reserved.

24

Unit 1 Test
Language: Usage and Practice 5, SV 1419027824

Unit 1 Test, p. 2

Darken the circle by the correct contraction for each pair of underlined words.

15. it is
(A) its
(B) its'
(C) i'ts
(D) it's

16. we had
(A) w'd
(B) w'ed
(C) we'ad
(D) we'd

17. they are
(A) the'yre
(B) the'are
(C) they're
(D) theyr'e

18. who would
(A) who'd
(B) who'wd
(C) who'uld
(D) who'ud

19. do not
(A) don'ot
(B) dont'
(C) do'not
(D) don't

20. she will
(A) shel'l
(B) shell'
(C) she'll
(D) sh'ell

Darken the circle by the two words that make up each underlined contraction.

21. I'll
(A) I would
(B) I did
(C) I have
(D) I will

22. they've
(A) they have
(B) they will
(C) they would
(D) they are

23. he'd
(A) he did
(B) he could
(C) he would
(D) he said

24. we're
(A) we were
(B) we are
(C) we have
(D) we will

Darken the circle by the word that combines with the word in parentheses to make a compound word that completes the sentence correctly.

25. The Dorn family lives on a (house) _____.
(A) shoe
(B) top
(C) boat
(D) branch

26. The bird was perched in the (tree) _____.
(A) trunk
(B) root
(C) top
(D) branch

27. I knew it was (some) _____ serious.
(A) matter
(B) thing
(C) day
(D) time

28. He held his breath (under) _____.
(A) way
(B) side
(C) ground
(D) water

29. I love (summer) _____.
(A) time
(B) sun
(C) vacation
(D) best

30. The handle on my (suit) _____ broke.
(A) coat
(B) case
(C) swim
(D) hanger

Language: Usage and Practice 5, SV 1419027824

Name _____   Date _____

What Is a Sentence?

- A **sentence** is a group of words that expresses a complete thought.
- A sentence always begins with a capital letter. It always ends with a punctuation mark.
- Every sentence has two parts. The **subject** is the part about which something is being said. The **predicate** tells about the subject.

    EXAMPLE:

Subject	**Predicate**
My fifth-grade class	is going on a field trip.

- The **complete subject** is all the words that make up the subject. A **simple subject** is the key word or words in the subject of a sentence. The simple subject tells whom or what the sentence is about.
- The **complete predicate** is a word or group of words that tells something about the subject. The **simple predicate** is the key word or words in the complete predicate. The simple predicate is an action verb or a linking verb, together with any helping verbs.

    EXAMPLES:

    A long, yellow school bus is taking us to New York.
    (complete subject)
    A long, yellow school **bus** is taking us to New York.
    (simple subject)
    Our teacher **sat up front**. (complete predicate)
    Our teacher **sat** up front. (simple predicate)

✼ **Add a complete subject or a complete predicate to each sentence.**

1. Mr. and Mrs. Brown _____.

2. _____ got off the bus in New York.

3. Tall buildings _____.

4. Some students _____.

5. The field trip _____.

6. _____ wants to go again soon.

7. Next time, the adults _____.

8. Before the second trip, they _____.

9. _____ will make the trip a success.

10. _____ had a good time on the field trip.

Unit 2: Sentences
Language: Usage and Practice 5, SV 1419027824

Name _____   Date _____

Recognizing Sentences

- A sentence is a group of words that expresses a complete thought.
    EXAMPLE: Many readers like stories about dogs.

✳ Some of the groups of words below are sentences, and some are not. Write <u>S</u> before each group that is a sentence.

_____ 1. One famous dog story.

_____ 2. First appeared in a well-known magazine.

_____ 3. You may have read this famous story.

_____ 4. A collie named Lassie, who was owned by a poor farmer in Yorkshire, England.

_____ 5. To make money for his family.

_____ 6. The farmer sold Lassie to a wealthy duke.

_____ 7. Lassie was loyal to her first master, however.

_____ 8. Taken hundreds of miles from Yorkshire.

_____ 9. She found her way back to her first home.

_____ 10. The story became a book and then a movie.

_____ 11. Helped two child actors on their way to stardom.

_____ 12. The real-life Lassie was a dog named Toots.

_____ 13. Toots was the companion of Eric Knight, the author of the story.

_____ 14. Lived in Yorkshire as a boy, but in the United States as an adult.

_____ 15. Knight died before his story, "Lassie Come Home," became famous.

_____ 16. Was killed in World War II.

_____ 17. Toots died on Knight's farm two years later.

✳ **Write a sentence about one of your favorite books.**

_____

_____

Unit 2: Sentences
Language: Usage and Practice 5, SV 1419027824

Name _____ Date _____

Types of Sentences

- A **declarative sentence** makes a statement.
  EXAMPLE: The telephone is ringing.
- An **interrogative sentence** asks a question.
  EXAMPLE: Where are you going?

✳ Write <u>declarative</u> or <u>interrogative</u> to describe each sentence in the conversation below.

1. When did you get those new skates? _____

2. I bought them yesterday. _____

3. Don't you think skating is dangerous? _____

4. It's not any more dangerous than skateboarding. _____

5. I would like to learn to skate. _____

6. Will you teach me? _____

7. Do you have a pair of skates? _____

8. No, but I will buy some tomorrow. _____

✳ Pretend that you are talking to the inventor of a new way to travel over land, sea, or in the air. Write four questions you'd ask and the inventor's answers. Label each sentence <u>D</u> for declarative or <u>I</u> for interrogative.

9. _____ _____

10. _____ _____

11. _____ _____

12. _____ _____

13. _____ _____

14. _____ _____

15. _____ _____

16. _____ _____

Unit 2: Sentences
Language: Usage and Practice 5, SV 1419027824

More Types of Sentences

> • An **imperative sentence** expresses a command or a request.
>   EXAMPLES: Answer the telephone.   Please don't shout.
> • An **exclamatory sentence** expresses strong or sudden feeling.
>   EXAMPLES: What a great movie!   They're off!

✳ Write <u>imperative</u> or <u>exclamatory</u> to describe each sentence.

1. Listen to that strange noise. _____

2. What a weird sound that is! _____

3. Go see what's there. _____

4. Go yourself. _____

5. I'm too scared! _____

6. Then look out the window. _____

7. What a cute kitten that is! _____

8. We shouldn't be scared! _____

9. Go get the kitten. _____

10. Come with me. _____

11. Oh, look! _____

12. Count the rest of the kittens in the basket. _____

13. Read the note attached to the handle. _____

14. What a surprise! _____

✳ **Write about a time you or someone you know was frightened by something. Use at least one exclamatory sentence and one imperative sentence.**

_____

_____

_____

_____

Language: Usage and Practice 5, SV 1419027824

Complete Subjects and Predicates

> - Every sentence has two main parts—a complete subject and a complete predicate.
> - The complete subject includes all the words that name the person, place, or thing about which something is said.
>   EXAMPLE: **My sister Sara** plays tennis.
> - The complete predicate includes all the words that tell what the subject is or does.
>   EXAMPLE: My sister Sara **plays tennis**.

✳ **Write S before each group of words that can be used as a complete subject. Write P before each group of words that can be used as a complete predicate.**

_____ 1. the mayor of our town

_____ 2. has a large town square

_____ 3. celebrate the holidays with parades

_____ 4. an election every four years

_____ 5. a map with every street in town

_____ 6. were planning to build a new swimming pool

✳ **Complete each sentence by writing a subject or a predicate.**

7. All our town council members _____.

8. _____ met in an important meeting.

9. _____ explained the problem.

10. Every interested citizen _____.

11. Our town's first settlers _____.

12. _____ planted crops.

13. _____ has been abandoned for years.

14. _____ should be preserved.

15. Some people _____.

16. _____ will have to come to vote.

17. My entire family _____.

Name _____   Date _____

Simple Subjects

> • The simple subject of a sentence is the main word in the complete subject.
>   EXAMPLE: **My friends** go mushroom hunting. The words <u>My friends</u> make up the complete subject. The word <u>friends</u> is the simple subject.
> • If the subject is made up of just one word, that word is both the complete subject and the simple subject.
>   EXAMPLE: **I** go mushroom hunting with my friends.

 In each sentence below, draw a line between the subject and the predicate. Underline the complete subject. Circle the simple subject.

1. <u>Freshly picked (morels)</u> are delicious.
2. These mushrooms can be found only in the spring.
3. A rich soil is best for morels.
4. Grassy spots are good places to look.
5. The spring must not be dry or too cold.
6. Damp earth is a good sign that morels may be found.
7. A clear, sunny sky means good hunting.
8. We never know where we'll find morels.
9. Tall, wet grasses often hide them.
10. We must work fast.
11. These spongy little mushrooms do not last long.
12. You might like to join us sometime.

 Write five sentences about an activity you enjoy. Draw a line between the subject and the predicate. Underline the complete subject. Circle the simple subject.

13. _____
14. _____
15. _____
16. _____
17. _____

Unit 2: Sentences
Language: Usage and Practice 5, SV 1419027824

Name _____   Date _____

Simple Predicates

- The simple predicate of a sentence is a verb within the complete predicate. The verb is an action or being word.
  - EXAMPLE: The Netherlands **attracts many tourists**. The words attracts many tourists make up the complete predicate. The verb attracts is the simple predicate.
- The simple predicate may be a one-word verb or a verb of more than one word.
  - EXAMPLES: Jan **likes** tulips. She **is planning** a garden.

 In each sentence below, draw a line between the subject and the predicate. Underline the complete predicate. Circle the simple predicate.

1. Many tourists visit the Netherlands in April or May.

2. The beautiful tulip blooms reach their height of glory during these months.

3. Visitors can see flowers for miles and miles.

4. Jan is dreaming of a trip to the Netherlands some day.

5. She has seen colorful pictures of tulips in catalogs.

6. The catalogs show tulips of all colors in full bloom.

7. Jan is eager to see the tulips herself.

8. Passing travelers can buy large bunches of flowers.

9. Every Dutch city has flowers everywhere.

10. Flower vases can be found in the cars of some Dutch people.

 Add a predicate for each subject below. Circle the simple predicate.

11. My neighbor's garden _____.

12. I _____.

13. All of the flowers _____.

 Write four sentences about a city or a country that you have visited or would like to visit. Draw a line between the subject and the predicate. Underline the complete predicate. Circle the simple predicate.

14. _____

15. _____

16. _____

17. _____

Understood Subjects

- The subject of an imperative sentence is always the person to whom the command or request is given (You).
- The subject does not appear in the sentence. Therefore, it is called an **understood subject**.
   EXAMPLES:
      (You) Keep off the grass. (You) Close the door, please.

✻ **On the line after each imperative sentence below, write the understood subject and the simple predicate.**

1. Turn left at the next light.   _____(You) Turn_____

2. Now turn right on Elm Street.   _____

3. Park in front of the house.   _____

4. Don't block the driveway.   _____

5. Leave enough room for them to leave.   _____

6. Help me with the food, please.   _____

7. Hold the door open until I get out.   _____

8. Get the bag off the back seat.   _____

9. Lock the car door, please.   _____

10. Check to see that the lights are off.   _____

11. Knock harder on the door.   _____

12. Try ringing the doorbell.   _____

✻ **Write four imperative sentences about a game or other activity. After each sentence, write the understood subject.**

13. _____

14. _____

15. _____

16. _____

Language: Usage and Practice 5, SV 1419027824

Name _____ Date _____

Using Compound Subjects

- Two sentences that have different subjects but the same predicate can be combined to make one sentence.
- The two subjects are joined by <u>and</u>.
- The subject of the new sentence is called a **compound subject**.
    EXAMPLE:
        Tom likes tall tales. **Jack** likes tall tales.
        Tom and Jack like tall tales.

✺ **In each sentence below, underline the subject. If the subject is compound, write <u>C</u> before the sentence.**

_____ 1. Paul Bunyan and Babe were the subject of many tall tales.

_____ 2. Babe was Paul's blue ox.

_____ 3. Maine and Minnesota are two of the states that have tall tales about Paul and Babe.

_____ 4. Babe could haul the timber from 640 acres at one time.

_____ 5. Lumberjacks and storytellers liked to tell tall tales about Paul and Babe's great deeds.

✺ **Combine each pair of sentences below to make a sentence that has a compound subject. Underline the compound subject.**

6. Tennessee claims Davy Crockett as its hero. Texas claims Davy Crockett as its hero.

_____

7. Great bravery made Davy Crockett famous. Unusual skills made Davy Crockett famous.

_____

8. True stories about Davy Crockett were passed down. Tall tales about Davy Crockett were passed down.

_____

9. These true stories made Davy Crockett a legend. These tall tales made Davy Crockett a legend.

_____

✺ **Write a sentence using <u>Paul Bunyan and Davy Crockett</u> as the subject.**

10. _____

_____

Language: Usage and Practice 5, SV 1419027824

Name _____ Date _____

Using Compound Predicates

- Two sentences that have the same subject but different predicates can be combined to make one sentence.
- The two predicates may be joined by or, and, or but.
- The predicate of the sentence is called a **compound predicate**.
  EXAMPLE:
  A newspaper **informs its readers**. A newspaper **entertains its readers**.
  A newspaper **informs and entertains its readers**.

❋ **In each sentence below, underline the predicate. If the predicate is compound, write C before the sentence.**

_____ 1. Our class wrote and printed its own newspaper.

_____ 2. Leslie was named editor-in-chief.

_____ 3. She assigned the stories and approved the final copies.

_____ 4. Wong and several other students were reporters.

_____ 5. They either wrote the news stories or edited the stories.

_____ 6. Wong interviewed a new student and wrote the interview.

❋ **Combine each pair of sentences below to make a sentence that has a compound predicate. Underline the compound predicate.**

7. Casey covered the baseball game. Casey described the best plays.

_____

8. Allison and Kim wrote jokes. Allison and Kim made up puzzles.

_____

9. Luis corrected the news stories. Luis wrote headlines.

_____

10. Alex typed the newspaper. Alex couldn't print the newspaper.

_____

❋ **Imagine that you are Casey. Write a sentence that has a compound predicate that could begin the story on the baseball game.**

11. _____

_____

Language: Usage and Practice 5, SV 1419027824

Name _____ Date _____

Simple and Compound Sentences

> - A **simple sentence** has one subject and one predicate.
>   EXAMPLE: <u>The United States' Presidents</u> / **led interesting lives**.
> - A **compound sentence** is made up of two simple sentences joined by connecting words such as <u>and</u>, <u>but</u>, and <u>or</u>. A comma is placed before the connecting word.
>   EXAMPLE: <u>George Washington</u> **led the army in the Revolutionary War**, and <u>Ulysses S. Grant</u> **led it in the Civil War**.

✳ **Draw a line between each subject and predicate. Write <u>S</u> before each simple sentence. Write <u>C</u> before each compound sentence.**

_____ 1. George Washington witnessed the first successful balloon flight.

_____ 2. John Adams was the second President, and his son was the sixth.

_____ 3. Thomas Jefferson was very interested in experiments with balloons and submarines.

_____ 4. The British burned the White House in 1814, but President Madison escaped unharmed.

✳ **Combine each pair of simple sentences below into a compound sentence.**

5. Andrew Jackson was called "Old Hickory."
   Zachary Taylor's nickname was "Old Rough and Ready."

   _____

   _____

6. Four presidents had no children. John Tyler had fourteen children.

   _____

   _____

7. Chester A. Arthur put the first bathroom in the White House.
   Benjamin Harrison put in electric lights.

   _____

   _____

8. Woodrow Wilson coached college football.
   Ronald Reagan announced baseball games on radio.

   _____

   _____

Language: Usage and Practice 5, SV 1419027824

Combining Sentences with the Same Subject or Predicate

- A good writer combines two or more sentences that have the same subject or predicate.
- The conjunctions <u>and</u>, <u>but</u>, and <u>or</u> are often used to combine sentence parts.
- When two sentences have the same predicate, the subjects can be combined.

  EXAMPLE:

  Theseus was angry. King Minos was angry.

  Theseus **and** King Minos were angry.
- When two sentences have the same subject, the predicates can be combined.

  EXAMPLE:

  Theseus found the ring. Theseus returned it.

  Theseus found the ring **and** returned it.

Rewrite this paragraph. Combine sentences with the same subjects or predicates to make it more interesting to read.

Each year, King Minos demanded a human sacrifice from the people of Athens. Seven boys would enter the Labyrinth. Seven girls would enter the Labyrinth. The Labyrinth was the home of the Minotaur. The Minotaur was half man. The Minotaur was half beast. The boys were devoured by the Minotaur. The girls were devoured by the Minotaur. Finally, Theseus found the Minotaur in the Labyrinth. Theseus killed the Minotaur in the Labyrinth.

_____

_____

_____

_____

_____

_____

_____

_____

Language: Usage and Practice 5, SV 1419027824

Name _____ Date _____

Combining Adjectives and Adverbs in Sentences

- To avoid short, choppy sentences, a writer often combines two or more sentences that describe the same subject.
- Sentences that describe the same subject with different adjectives can sometimes be combined.
   EXAMPLE:
   Tara was **diligent**. She was also **courageous**.
   Tara was **diligent and courageous**.
- Sentences that describe the same verb with different adverbs can also be combined.
   EXAMPLE:
   William studied **eagerly**. He studied **carefully**.
   William studied **eagerly and carefully**.

✳ **Combine each set of sentences to make one sentence. Then tell if you combined adjectives or adverbs.**

1. Lashonda waited patiently. She waited quietly. _____

   _____

2. She had felt disappointed before. She had felt rejected before. _____

   _____

3. She really wanted to be a scientist. She truly wanted to be a scientist. ___

   _____

4. Lashonda read the letter slowly. She read the letter calmly. _____

   _____

5. She was happy about the news. She was excited about the news. _____

   _____

6. She spread the news happily. She spread the news quickly. _____

   _____

7. Her parents were proud. Her parents were excited. _____

   _____

8. Lashonda began to pack quickly. She began to pack carefully. _____

   _____

Language: Usage and Practice 5, SV 1419027824

Name _____   Date _____

Joining Sentences

- A writer can join two short, choppy sentences into one that is more interesting to read. The result is a compound sentence.
- Use the conjunction <u>and</u> to join two sentences that show addition or similarity.
  EXAMPLE:
  Patrick saw the house. He decided it was haunted.
  Patrick saw the house, **and** he decided it was haunted.
- Use the conjunction <u>but</u> to join two sentences that show contrast.
  EXAMPLE:
  Patrick ran up the steps. He stopped at the door.
  Patrick ran up the steps, **but** he stopped at the door.
- Use the conjunction <u>or</u> to join two sentences that show choice.
  EXAMPLE:
  Should he go inside? Should he explore outside?
  Should he go inside, **or** should he explore outside?

 Join each pair of sentences. Use the conjunctions <u>and</u>, <u>but</u>, or <u>or</u>.

1. Patrick studied the wall. He found a hidden button.

   _____

2. Patrick pushed the button. The bookcase moved.

   _____

3. Patrick could wait. He could explore the path.

   _____

4. He wasn't afraid. He wasn't comfortable, either.

   _____

5. Patrick thought about what to do. He decided to explore.

   _____

6. The path was dark. Patrick felt nervous.

   _____

7. He started down the path. He stopped when he heard a noise.

   _____

Sentence Variety

> - To add variety to sentences, a writer sometimes changes the order of the words.
> - Usually the subject comes before the verb. This is called **natural order**.
>   EXAMPLE:
>   Angela led Jacob down a twisting path.
> - Sometimes the subject and verb can be reversed. This is called **inverted order**.
>   EXAMPLE:
>   At the end of the path was a small shack.

 Write each sentence, changing the word order whenever doing so will not change the meaning. Tell which sentences cannot be changed and explain why.

1. On the little door shone the sunlight.

   _____

2. Angela and Jacob walked into the shack.

   _____

3. Inside the shack was a large wooden table.

   _____

4. On the table lay a black cat.

   _____

5. Angela reached out to the cat.

   _____

6. At work in the shack was a witch's magic!

   _____

7. Angela told Jacob to follow her out.

   _____

8. Out the door went the two friends.

   _____

Language: Usage and Practice 5, SV 1419027824

Avoiding Sentence Fragments
and Run-on Sentences

- To avoid writing **sentence fragments**, be sure each sentence has a subject and a predicate and expresses a complete thought.
- To avoid writing **run-on sentences**, be sure you join two complete sentences with a comma and a **conjunction**. You may also write them as two separate sentences.

 Read each group of words. If it is a correct simple sentence, write simple sentence on the line. If it is a sentence fragment or a run-on sentence, rewrite it correctly.

1. A box turtle is a reptile it lives in woods and fields.

   _____

2. The box turtle has a hinged lower shell.

   _____

3. Can pull its legs, head, and tail inside its shell and get "boxed in."

   _____

   _____

4. Many kinds of turtles on land and in the water.

   _____

5. Belong to the same family as lizards, snakes, alligators, and crocodiles.

   _____

   _____

6. Box turtles will eat earthworms, insects, berries, and green leafy vegetables.

   _____

7. Painted turtles eat meal worms, earthworms, minnows, and insects the musk turtle finds food along the bottoms of ponds or streams.

   _____

   _____

   _____

8. Painted turtles get their name from the red and yellow patterns on their shell they also have yellow lines on their head.

   _____

   _____

Language: Usage and Practice 5, SV 1419027824

Name ______________________________ Date ____________________

Correcting Run-on Sentences

- Two or more sentences that are run together without the correct punctuation are called a **run-on sentence**.
  EXAMPLE: Animals that carry their young in the mother's pouch are called marsupials, they live mainly in Australia.
- Correct a run-on sentence by making separate sentences from its parts.
  EXAMPLE: Animals that carry their young in the mother's pouch are called marsupials. They live mainly in Australia.

Separate the run-on sentences below. Rewrite the sentences to make them correct.

1. There are over two hundred kinds of marsupials all live in North or South America or in Australia. ______________________________

____

2. The kangaroo is the largest marsupial, the male red kangaroo may be up to seven feet tall. ______________________________

____

3. Wallabies are similar to kangaroos, they are smaller than kangaroos, some are the size of a rabbit. ______________________________

____

4. Kangaroos and wallabies live only in Australia, their hind feet are larger than their front feet. ______________________________

____

Correct the run-on sentences in the paragraph below. Rewrite the paragraph so that no run-on sentences remain. Use another piece of paper if necessary.

Opossums are the only marsupials that live north of Mexico, they also live in Central and South America. Opossums are grayish white, they have a long snout, hairless ears, and a long, hairless tail. Opossums have fifty teeth, the opossum mother has from five to twenty babies, each baby is the size of a kidney bean.

____

____

____

Name _____ Date _____

Unit 2 Test

Darken the circle by the group of words that is a sentence.

1. Ⓐ A huge map of the town.
   Ⓑ I located the school on the map.
   Ⓒ Couldn't find my house.
   Ⓓ Where is?

2. Ⓐ So could meet.
   Ⓑ Before we leave.
   Ⓒ Saw us last week!
   Ⓓ Jim plays the piano.

Decide whether each sentence is declarative, interrogative, imperative, or exclamatory. Darken the circle by your choice.

3. How did Ryan injure his thumb?
   Ⓐ declarative
   Ⓑ interrogative
   Ⓒ imperative
   Ⓓ exclamatory

5. Get a bandage for Ryan.
   Ⓐ declarative
   Ⓑ interrogative
   Ⓒ imperative
   Ⓓ exclamatory

4. He cut it on a tin can.
   Ⓐ declarative
   Ⓑ interrogative
   Ⓒ imperative
   Ⓓ exclamatory

6. What a bad cut it was!
   Ⓐ declarative
   Ⓑ interrogative
   Ⓒ imperative
   Ⓓ exclamatory

Darken the circle by the part of each sentence that is underlined.

7. The seasons are four parts of a year.
   Ⓐ simple subject
   Ⓑ simple predicate
   Ⓒ complete subject
   Ⓓ complete predicate

9. Winter makes some people sad.
   Ⓐ simple subject
   Ⓑ simple predicate
   Ⓒ complete subject
   Ⓓ complete predicate

8. Spring and summer are warm.
   Ⓐ simple subject
   Ⓑ simple predicate
   Ⓒ complete subject
   Ⓓ complete predicate

10. Other people feel just the opposite.
    Ⓐ simple subject
    Ⓑ simple predicate
    Ⓒ complete subject
    Ⓓ complete predicate

Language: Usage and Practice 5, SV 1419027824

Unit 2 Test, p. 2

Darken the circle by the correct answer to each question.

11. In which sentence is the simple subject underlined?

Ⓐ My <u>friend</u> has a neat workshop.

Ⓑ He has <u>all kinds</u> of tools.

Ⓒ <u>My favorite tool</u> is the jigsaw.

Ⓓ Joe and I <u>cut</u> pieces for puzzles.

12. In which sentence is the complete predicate underlined?

Ⓐ <u>Kimberly</u> joined the band.

Ⓑ She <u>can</u> play the drums.

Ⓒ Our band marched <u>in a parade</u>.

Ⓓ My little brother <u>waved to me</u>.

13. In which sentence is the compound predicate underlined?

Ⓐ All living things <u>grow and die</u>.

Ⓑ Animals and plants <u>breathe differently</u>.

Ⓒ Some <u>plants and animals</u> can live underwater.

Ⓓ Others <u>must</u> live on land.

14. In which sentence is the compound subject underlined?

Ⓐ Ted <u>finished wrapping</u> the package.

Ⓑ <u>Ribbons and bows</u> made it colorful.

Ⓒ He used <u>glue</u> and tape.

Ⓓ It was very <u>hard for Erin</u> to open.

Darken the circle by the sentence that is the best combination of the two simple sentences.

15. The planet Mercury doesn't have any moons. Venus doesn't have any moons.

Ⓐ Mercury is a planet, and so is Venus.

Ⓑ Mercury has no moons, neither does Venus.

Ⓒ Mercury and Venus do not have any moons.

Ⓓ Mercury and Venus have moons, but we can't see them.

16. Venus is similar to Earth. Venus is hotter than Earth.

Ⓐ Venus is different from Earth.

Ⓑ Earth is colder than Venus.

Ⓒ Venus is similar to Earth, but it is hotter.

Ⓓ Venus and Earth are the same size.

Darken the circle by the answer that correctly describes each sentence.

17. The driver pulled over, and then he stopped.

Ⓐ simple

Ⓑ compound

Ⓒ run-on

Ⓓ not a sentence

18. He avoided an accident.

Ⓐ simple

Ⓑ compound

Ⓒ run-on

Ⓓ not a sentence

Name _____ Date _____

Nouns

> • A **noun** is a word that names a person, place, thing, or quality.
> EXAMPLES: Rachel, city, Montana, shell, animal, happiness

Write nouns that name the following:

1. Four people you admire

   _____   _____

   _____   _____

2. Four places you would like to visit

   _____   _____

   _____   _____

3. Six things you use every day

   _____   _____

   _____   _____

   _____   _____

4. Four qualities you would like to have

   _____   _____

   _____   _____

5. Four states in the United States

   _____   _____

   _____   _____

Find and underline 26 nouns in the sentences below.

6. Every section of the United States has scenes of natural beauty.
7. The tall trees in California are called the giants of the forest.
8. Every fall, tourists go to see the colorful trees in Vermont.
9. Southern coastal cities are proud of their sandy beaches.
10. Colorful flowers and grasses cover the prairies of Texas.
11. Montana and Wyoming have majestic mountains.
12. The citizens of every state take pride in the charm of their own state.

Unit 3: Grammar and Usage
Language: Usage and Practice 5, SV 1419027824

Common and Proper Nouns

- There are two main classes of nouns: common and proper nouns.
- A **common noun** is a word that names any one of a class of objects. A common noun begins with a lowercase letter.
  EXAMPLES: girl, city, dog
- A **proper noun** is the name of a particular person, place, or thing. It begins with a capital letter.
  EXAMPLES: Shari, Nashville, Digger

✳ **Write a proper noun for each common noun below.**

1. city _____
2. school _____
3. friend _____
4. ocean _____
5. state _____
6. car _____
7. singer _____
8. day _____
9. lake _____

10. street _____
11. game _____
12. river _____
13. woman _____
14. country _____
15. man _____
16. movie star _____
17. month _____
18. planet _____

✳ **Write a common noun for each proper noun below.**

19. Alaska _____
20. November _____
21. Thanksgiving _____
22. Karla _____
23. December _____
24. Hawaii _____
25. *Call of the Wild* _____
26. Saturday _____
27. Hudson Bay _____

28. South America _____
29. Dr. Cooke _____
30. Rocky Mountains _____
31. Abraham Lincoln _____
32. Sahara _____
33. Denver _____
34. Mexico _____
35. Saturn _____
36. Jason _____

Singular and Plural Nouns

> • A **singular noun** is a noun that names one person, place, or thing.
>   EXAMPLES: knife, church, boy, mouse
> • A **plural noun** is a noun that names more than one person, place, or thing.
>   EXAMPLES: knives, churches, boys, mice

✳ Write S before each singular noun below. Then write its plural form. Write P before each plural noun. Then write its singular form. You may wish to check the spellings in a dictionary.

_____ 1. boots _____   _____ 9. baby _____

_____ 2. army _____   _____ 10. women _____

_____ 3. match _____   _____ 11. halves _____

_____ 4. maps _____   _____ 12. skies _____

_____ 5. inches _____   _____ 13. wife _____

_____ 6. foot _____   _____ 14. boxes _____

_____ 7. hero _____   _____ 15. beach _____

_____ 8. alley _____   _____ 16. book _____

✳ Write the plural form of each word below to complete the sentences.

| watch   shelf   child   story   monkey   player |

17. There are many interesting _____ in that magazine.

18. The cover story on timepieces describes the making of _____.

19. A sports story contains conversations with three of the nation's leading football

_____.

20. A do-it-yourself article shows how to build _____ that will hold an aquarium.

21. Unusual _____ and apes are shown in a picture story.

22. This month's special article is a selection of poems and stories by German

_____.

Name _____ Date _____

Special Plural Nouns

> • Some nouns change spelling in the plural form.
> • Other nouns have the same singular and plural form.
>   EXAMPLES:
>
> | Change Spelling | Same Singular and Plural |
> |---|---|
> | woman—women | salmon |
> | child—children | elk |
> | tooth—teeth | deer |
> | goose—geese | trout |
> | hoof—hooves | sheep |

✳ **Complete each sentence by writing the plural form of the noun in parentheses.**

1. Lisa caught four special _____ in that stream.
   (trout)

2. These _____ told Lisa a story.
   (fish)

3. They said that they were really _____.
   (hero)

4. Two of them were really _____.
   (woman)

5. The other two were really _____.
   (man)

6. They had chased out all the _____ from their village.
   (mouse)

7. This went against the _____ of the other people in the village.
   (belief)

8. The village people thought mice protected them from _____.
   (wolf)

9. For a while, they had been four _____ in a field.
   (ox)

10. Then they had been turned into _____ in a barnyard.
    (calf)

11. Later they were changed into _____.
    (goose)

12. All the _____ in the village made fun of them.
    (child)

13. Finally, their _____ were turned into fins.
    (foot)

14. If they could eat bread, their _____ would return to normal.
    (life)

Language: Usage and Practice 5, SV 1419027824

Singular Possessive Nouns

- A **possessive noun** shows possession of the noun that follows.
  EXAMPLES: mother's car   the dog's bone
- To form the possessive of most singular nouns, add an **apostrophe (')** and s.
  EXAMPLES: Adriana's room   the city's mayor

✳ **Write the possessive form of the noun in parentheses to complete each phrase.**

1. the _____ leash (dog)

2. the _____ lawn (neighbor)

3. one of the _____ engines (plane)

4. _____ greatest ambition (Ann)

5. to_____ house (grandmother)

6. the _____ paw (tiger)

7. my _____ farm (sister)

8. your _____ best friend (brother)

9. our _____ advice (mother)

10. that _____ tires (truck)

11. my _____ apple (teacher)

12. that _____ fur (cat)

13. the _____ teeth (dinosaur)

14. the _____ coach (team)

✳ **Write each of the phrases below in a shorter way.**

15. the friend of Amanda   _Amanda's friend_____

16. the car of the friend   _____

17. the director of the play   _____

18. the roar of the lion   _____

19. the growl of the tiger   _____

Unit 3: Grammar and Usage
Language: Usage and Practice 5, SV 1419027824

Name _____   Date _____

Plural Possessive Nouns

- To form the possessive of a plural noun ending in <u>s</u>, add only an apostrophe.
  EXAMPLES: the boys' coats   the books' covers
- To form the possessive of a plural noun that does not end in <u>s</u>, add an **apostrophe (')** and <u>s</u>.
  EXAMPLES: men's suits   children's toys

✳ **Complete the chart below. You may wish to check the spellings in a dictionary.**

Singular noun	Plural noun	Singular possessive	Plural possessive
1. horse	horses	horse's	horses'
2. bird			
3. teacher			
4. child			
5. truck			
6. doctor			
7. man			
8. church			

✳ **Rewrite each sentence using a possessive noun.**

9. <u>The cat of the Smiths</u> has three kittens.

_____

10. <u>The names of the kittens</u> are Frisky, Midnight, and Puff.

_____

11. <u>The dogs of the neighbors</u> are very playful.

_____

12. <u>The pen of the dogs</u> is in the yard.

_____

13. <u>The curiosity of the cats</u> might get them into trouble.

_____

Name _____   Date _____

Action Verbs

> • A **verb** is a word that shows action. The verb may show action that can be seen.
>   EXAMPLE: Jane **opened** the door.
> • The verb may show action that cannot be seen.
>   EXAMPLE: Mary **thought** about her lunch.

 Underline the verb in each sentence. The first one is done for you.

1. Several years ago people <u>started</u> recycling materials.
2. Today people recycle many things.
3. They buy special containers to sort their wastes.
4. In years past, few people recycled.
5. People threw most of their trash away.
6. Some people burned their trash.
7. This harmed the environment.
8. Then groups of people asked companies to recycle used materials.
9. Today many companies recycle materials.
10. People throw less trash away.
11. Many groups work hard to encourage recycling.
12. Responsible companies now recycle many things.

Complete each sentence with one of the verbs in the box. Use each verb once.

believe	felt	hoped	knew	remember	studied	thought	worried

13. Yoko really _____ about the math test.
14. She _____ every day.
15. She _____ she could pass the test.
16. During the test, Yoko _____ carefully about each problem.
17. Could she _____ all she had studied?
18. She _____ more confident once the test was over.
19. She _____ that she had done well.
20. When Yoko got her test back, she couldn't _____ she got an A!

Action Verbs and Linking Verbs

- A verb expresses action or being.
- An **action verb** is a word or group of words that expresses an action. An action verb is often the key word in the predicate. It tells what the subject does.
- A **linking verb** connects the subject of a sentence with a word or words in the predicate.
- The most common linking verb is be. Some forms of be are am, is, are, was, and were.
- Other common linking verbs are become, feel, seem, look, grow, taste, appear, and smell.

      EXAMPLES:
          King Uther **ruled** England a long time ago. (action)
          The name of his baby boy **was** Arthur. (linking)
          In time, Sir Ector **became** Arthur's guardian. (linking)

 Read each sentence. Underline each action verb. Circle each linking verb.

1. Young Arthur felt very nervous.

2. Sir Kay left his sword at the inn.

3. He needed his sword for the tournament that day.

4. Arthur looked all over the village for a replacement.

5. Suddenly, Arthur saw a sword in a stone.

6. He ran over to the stone and studied the strange sword.

7. It appeared very secure in its stony sheath.

8. Arthur pulled it, and it moved.

9. The sword slid from the stone easily!

10. Arthur hurried back to the tournament with his prize.

11. Sir Ector bowed deeply to his foster son.

12. The sword was the sign of the next king of England.

13. The young boy was now King Arthur.

14. He was a good and wise king.

Name _____ Date _____

Helping Verbs

- A verb may have a **main verb** and one or more **helping verbs**.
- Such a verb is called a **verb phrase**.
  EXAMPLES:
  The bells **were ringing**.
  Where **have** you **been hiding**?

 Underline each main verb. Circle each helping verb. Some verbs do not have a helping verb.

1. (Have) you <u>heard</u> of Casey Jones?
2. He was born John Luther Jones in Cayce, Kentucky.
3. As a railroad engineer, he could make sad music with his locomotive whistle.
4. Soon people were telling stories about Casey.
5. One of the stories was about his train wreck.
6. One day he had climbed into his engine cab.
7. The train was carrying the mail.
8. It had been pouring rain for more than a week.
9. The railroad track was covered with water.
10. They were running late.
11. But maybe they could make it on time!
12. Around a curve, they saw a passenger train.
13. Everyone jumped.
14. But Casey did his job, faithful and true to the end.
15. People still sing about this brave railroad man.

 Complete each sentence by adding <u>have</u>, <u>will</u>, or <u>would</u>.

16. Maria and Ricardo _____ like to go swimming.
17. They _____ received permission from their parents.
18. This _____ be their second trip to the pool today.
19. They _____ be tired after all this swimming.
20. Their cousins _____ like to join them at the pool.

Language: Usage and Practice 5, SV 1419027824

Name _____   Date _____

Present and Past Tense

> • A verb in the **present tense** shows an action that happens now.
>   EXAMPLE: I **watch** TV.
> • A verb in the **past tense** shows an action that happened in the past.
>   EXAMPLE: I **watched** TV.

 Underline each verb in the present tense.

1. A famous poem tells about another Casey.
2. This Casey plays baseball.
3. His great skill with the bat makes him a hero.
4. The people in the town of Mudville call him the Mighty Casey.
5. Casey is one of the greatest players.
6. He frightens pitchers.
7. He often hits the winning run for his team.
8. The fans love Casey.

 Underline each verb or verb phrase in the past tense.

9. The game had reached the last inning.
10. The Mudville team trailed four to two.
11. The first two batters were called out at first base.
12. Many in the crowd left the game and went home.
13. But the next two men up made hits.
14. Then Casey came up to the plate.
15. The crowd went wild.
16. But the Mighty Casey struck out.

 List four verbs you know.

present tense	past tense
17.	
18.	
19.	
20.	

Language: Usage and Practice 5, SV 1419027824

Name _____   Date _____

Irregular Verbs

- An **irregular verb** is a verb that does not end with <u>ed</u> to show past tense.
- Some irregular verbs show past tense by using a different form of the main verb with <u>have</u>, <u>has</u>, or <u>had</u>.

EXAMPLES:
Present	Past	Past with Helping Verb
do, does	did	(have, has, had) done
come, comes	came	(have, has, had) come
run, runs	ran	(have, has, had) run
go, goes	went	(have, has, had) gone

 Write the past-tense form of the verb in parentheses that correctly completes each sentence.

1. Ashley has _____ a report on chameleons.
   (do)

2. She _____ a bus to the zoo to do research.
   (ride)

3. She _____ some change to the bus driver.
   (give)

4. At the zoo, Ashley _____ from the entrance to the lizard area.
   (run)

5. The chameleons had _____ out into the sunlight.
   (come)

6. She _____ her lunch and watched the lizards.
   (eat)

7. She _____ several chameleons, each a different color.
   (see)

8. The guide had _____ hello to her.
   (say)

9. Ashley _____ twelve photos of the reptiles for her report.
   (take)

10. She had _____ about her report for weeks.
    (think)

11. She had _____ a rough draft already.
    (write)

12. That afternoon, she _____ home and worked on the report.
    (go)

13. She _____ the report a lot of thought.
    (give)

14. She _____ a good job on the report.
    (do)

Language: Usage and Practice 5, SV 1419027824

More Irregular Verbs

- Remember that an irregular verb is a verb that does not end with **ed** to show past tense.
- Some irregular verbs use **n** or **en** to form the past tense.

 Write the past-tense form of the verb in parentheses that correctly completes each sentence.

1. Wesley _____ a study of Japan last week.
(begin)

2. One of his mother's friends _____ up in Japan.
(grow)

3. Wesley has _____ his mother's friend for many years.
(know)

4. Jinko had _____ to come to America long ago.
(choose)

5. She had always _____ fondly of her home.
(speak)

6. Last year Jinko _____ to Japan to visit family and friends.
(fly)

7. Jinko had _____ a kimono at her wedding.
(wear)

8. Once she _____ the pictures of her wedding.
(lose)

9. She _____ them again last year.
(find)

10. Her dog had _____ a few of them.
(tear)

11. One afternoon, Wesley's doorbell _____.
(ring)

12. Wesley had _____ a cold and had missed school.
(catch)

13. He had _____ in a pool on a cool evening.
(swim)

14. Jinko _____ some Japanese music to Wesley's house.
(bring)

15. She _____ some Japanese songs for Wesley's mother.
(sing)

Name _____ Date _____

Future Tense

- A verb in the **future tense** shows an action that will happen at some time in the future.
- The helping verb <u>will</u> is used with the present tense form of the verb.
  EXAMPLE: I will meet you tomorrow.

✻ **Write a verb in the future tense to complete each sentence.**

1. Kayla _____ the invitations.

2. Dina and Andrew _____ what games to play.

3. We all _____ the balloons with air.

4. Matt and Ella _____ the table decorations.

5. Carlos and Rosa _____ the cake.

6. Chris _____ of a way to get Flash to come over.

7. We all _____ in the back room.

8. When Chris and Flash come in, everyone _____, "Surprise!"

✻ **The sentences below show an event that happened in the past. Rewrite each underlined verb to change the event to a time in the future.**

9. Caree <u>sent</u> a letter to the Round-the-World Travel Agency. _____

10. She <u>received</u> an answer in a day or two. _____

11. The agency <u>mailed</u> her folders containing information about exciting places to visit. _____

12. Caree <u>studied</u> the information. _____

13. She <u>chose</u> to write about three places. _____

14. Then she <u>planned</u> an imaginary trip to those three places. _____

15. She <u>wrote</u> in detail about her imaginary trip. _____

16. She <u>designed</u> her report with pictures from the travel agency folders. _____

17. She <u>made</u> an interesting cover for her report. _____

18. Then she <u>hoped</u> for a good grade. _____

Subject-Verb Agreement

- A **singular subject** must have a **singular verb**.
  EXAMPLES:
  <u>Jane</u> **lives** there.
  <u>She</u> **does** not **live** near me.
- A **plural subject** must have a **plural verb**.
  EXAMPLES:
  <u>Jane and her sister</u> **live** there.
  <u>They</u> **do** not **live** near me.
- <u>You</u> and <u>I</u> must have a plural verb.

 Write <u>S</u> over each singular subject. Write <u>P</u> over each plural subject. Then underline the correct verb in parentheses.

1. Many stories (tell, tells) how dogs become friends of people.

2. A story by Rudyard Kipling (say, says) that Wild Dog agreed to help hunt and guard in exchange for bones.

3. After that, Wild Dog (become, becomes) First Friend.

4. Many dogs never (leave, leaves) their masters.

5. In another story, a dog (doesn't, don't) leave his master's dead body and dies in the Arctic cold.

6. There are few people in history that (doesn't, don't) record the usefulness of dogs.

7. Diggings in Egypt (prove, proves) that the dog was a companion in ancient Egypt.

8. Bones of dogs (does, do) appear in Egyptian graves.

9. Ancient Greek vases (picture, pictures) dogs on them.

10. Today the Leader Dog organization (train, trains) dogs to guide people who can't see.

11. One man who can't see said, "My eyes (have, has) a wet nose."

12. A dog (does, do) have excellent hearing and smelling abilities.

13. What person (doesn't, don't) agree that a dog is a person's best friend?

14. Dogs (is, are) very loyal companions.

15. When I come home after a hard day, my dog always (bring, brings) a smile to my face.

Agreement with Linking Verbs

- A **linking verb** is a verb that joins the subject of a sentence with a word in the predicate.
  EXAMPLES: Bob **is** an artist. Bob **was** late.
- A singular subject must have a singular linking verb.
  EXAMPLES: Maria **is** a singer. Maria **was** happy.
- A plural subject must have a plural linking verb.
  EXAMPLES: Becka and Lynn **are** sisters. The sisters **were** happy.
- <u>You</u> must have a plural linking verb.

 Write <u>S</u> over each singular subject. Write <u>P</u> over each plural subject. Then circle the correct linking verb.

1. Tracy (is, are) a clown.

2. Her brothers (is, are) acrobats.

3. Tracy and her brothers (was, were) in a show.

4. Tracy (was, were) funny.

5. Her brothers (was, were) daring.

6. The people watching (was, were) delighted.

7. Tracy (was, were) amusing with her big red nose.

8. Tracy's brothers (was, were) high in the air on a swing.

9. (Was, Were) you ever at their show?

10. Tracy (is, are) glad that I went to see her perform.

Circle the correct linking verb in parentheses.

11. Ice skating (is, are) a popular winter sport today.

12. (Isn't, Aren't) there a skating rink or pond in every northern town?

13. Even in many southern towns, there (is, are) an indoor rink.

14. The discovery of ice skating (were, was) an accident.

15. An Arctic settler who slipped on a piece of bone and skidded across the ice (was, were) the inventor of the ice skate.

16. Pieces of bone attached to his feet (was, were) the first ice skates.

17. Now we (is, are) all able to enjoy his invention.

18. That (was, were) a lucky day for all ice skaters!

19. Ice skating (is, are) a popular Olympic sport.

20. Olympic ice skaters (is, are) excellent athletes.

Name _____ Date _____

Forms of *Go, Do, See,* and *Sing*

> • Never use a helping verb with <u>went</u>, <u>did</u>, <u>saw</u>, or <u>sang</u>.
>   EXAMPLES: Soo-Lee **did** her work. Sam **went** home. Sara **sang** a song.
> • Always use a helping verb with <u>gone</u>, <u>done</u>, <u>seen</u>, or <u>sung</u>.
>   EXAMPLES: Sara **has done** her work. Marcy **had** not **seen** me.

❋ **Circle the correct verb in parentheses.**

1. The class members (did, done) very well on their music project.

2. Most of them had (gone, went) to extra practices.

3. They (sang, sung) at the special spring concert.

4. The class had (sang, sung) in the concert before, but they (did, done) even better this year.

5. The teacher said she had never (saw, seen) a class work so well together.

6. The teacher said they had (sang, sung) beautifully.

7. They (sang, sung) so well that she was very proud of them.

8. The week after the concert, the class (gone, went) to a music museum.

9. The trip was a reward because the class had (did, done) so well.

10. The class (saw, seen) pictures of famous musicians at the museum.

11. After they had (saw, seen) an exhibit of unusual music boxes, they wished the boxes were for sale.

12. What do you think the teacher (did, done)?

13. She took the class to a music shop she had (gone, went) to before.

14. The teacher and the shop owner had (sang, sung) together.

15. They had (gone, went) to the same music school.

16. So the class (went, gone) to this shop and saw many little musical toys.

17. In the shop they (saw, seen) many small music boxes.

❋ **Write the correct form of each verb in parentheses.**

18. (go)   Kate has _____ to voice class.

19. (do)   She has _____ that every day for a year.

20. (see)   Her friends have _____ her sing in public.

21. (sing)   She _____ last week at the auditorium.

Language: Usage and Practice 5, SV 1419027824

Name _____ Date _____

Forms of *Break, Drink, Take,* and *Write*

- Never use a helping verb with <u>broke</u>, <u>drank</u>, <u>took</u>, or <u>wrote</u>.
  EXAMPLES: Kim **broke** her arm.   Jack **wrote** a letter.
- Always use a helping verb with <u>broken</u>, <u>drunk</u>, <u>taken</u>, or <u>written</u>.
  EXAMPLES: Kim **has broken** her arm.   Jack **had written** a note.

✳ **Complete each sentence with the correct form of one of the verbs below.**

broke, broken	drank, drunk	took, taken	wrote, written

1. Rick _____ his time writing the letter.

2. He had _____ Amber's sculpture from her, and he needed to apologize.

3. He _____ slowly and carefully, thinking hard about each word.

4. Whenever he paused, he _____ sips of water from the glass on his desk.

5. In the letter, he said he was sorry he had _____ the sculpture.

6. Although he tried to be careful, he _____ it.

7. He _____ that he would never do anything like that again.

8. Then he read what he had _____.

9. He saw that he had _____ all of his water.

10. It had _____ all his courage to write that letter.

✳ **Write the correct form of each verb in parentheses.**

11. (take)   Alana had _____ her dog for a long walk and was thirsty.

12. (drink)   So she had _____ a glass of fruit juice.

13. (break)   She was careful and had not _____ the glass.

14. (break)   But then her dog, Daisy, had _____ it.

15. (write)   Now Alana has _____ a note of apology.

Name _____ Date _____

Forms of *Eat, Draw, Give,* and *Ring*

- Never use a helping verb with <u>ate</u>, <u>drew</u>, <u>gave</u>, or <u>rang</u>.
  EXAMPLES: Ann **ate** her lunch.   The telephone **rang**.
- Always use a helping verb with <u>eaten</u>, <u>drawn</u>, <u>given</u>, or <u>rung</u>.
  EXAMPLES: Ann **has eaten** her lunch.   The telephone **has rung**.

✳ **Complete each sentence with the correct form of the verb in parentheses.**

1. (give)   Amanda _____ samples of the granola bars she had made to three of her friends.

2. (eat)   The bars were soon _____, and there were cries of "More!"

3. (eat)   "You _____ those already?" Amanda asked.

4. (give)   "I should have _____ you the recipe."

5. (eat)   "Please do!" said her friends. "We have never _____ anything so delicious."

6. (give)   "I _____ them to you for your health's sake," said Amanda.

7. (ring)   Just then the telephone _____.

8. (draw)   "Hello," said Amanda. "You have _____ my name?"

9. (draw)   "They _____ my name as the winner!" she told her friends.

10. (ring)   "If that phone hadn't _____ when it did, we would have gone home," said Paul.

11. (eat)   "If you had _____ any faster, you would have missed all the excitement," said Amanda.

✳ **Circle the correct verb in parentheses.**

12. The telephone has just (rang, rung).
13. Carla and Sadie have (eat, eaten) breakfast and are looking for something to do.
14. Now Jerome has (gave, given) them a call to ask if they would like to come to his house.
15. He has (drew, drawn) a sketch that he wants to show them.
16. They have (gave, given) him feedback on his sketches before.
17. The last sketch Jerome (drew, drawn) won first prize in the school art contest.

Unit 3: Grammar and Usage
Language: Usage and Practice 5, SV 1419027824

Forms of *Begin, Fall, Steal,* and *Throw*

> • Never use a helping verb with began, fell, stole, or threw.
>   EXAMPLES: Tina **began** to run.   Juan **fell** down.
> • Always use a helping verb with begun, fallen, stolen, or thrown.
>   EXAMPLES: Tina had begun to run.   Juan had fallen.

 Circle the correct verb in parentheses.

1. Spring baseball practice had just (began, begun).

2. The pitchers on the Blasters' team had (threw, thrown) a few balls.

3. The other Blasters (began, begun) to practice.

4. They would need much practice because they had (fell, fallen) into last place at the end of last season.

5. The Blasters' coaches (threw, thrown) themselves into their work.

6. The biggest job (fell, fallen) on the batting and base-running coach.

7. The team batting average had (fell, fallen) out of sight.

8. And the players had (stole, stolen) only forty bases last year.

9. One runner (stole, stolen) three bases in one game.

10. The coach said, "Our team motto will be 'We have just (began, begun) to fight!'"

11. With that, the Blasters (fell, fallen) to work.

12. The pitchers (threw, thrown) many different kinds of pitches.

13. The fastest pitch was (threw, thrown) at ninety miles per hour.

14. The batters were hitting everything that was (threw, thrown) to them.

 Write the correct form of each verb in parentheses.

15. (steal)   In last night's opening game, Nick, our team's fastest base runner, had

    _____ home.

16. (begin)   We had _____ to warm up Willis, our relief pitcher, before
    the sixth inning.

17. (throw)   He had _____ the ball so well last year that no batters could
    hit his pitches.

18. (begin)   After Willis won last night's game for us, we told him that he had

    _____ our season in great style.

Language: Usage and Practice 5, SV 1419027824

Name _____   Date _____

Direct Objects

> • A **direct object** is a noun or pronoun that receives the action of the verb.
> • Use object pronouns such as <u>me</u>, <u>you</u>, <u>him</u>, <u>her</u>, <u>it</u>, <u>us</u>, and <u>them</u> as direct objects.
>   EXAMPLES:
>   The country of France gave the **Statue of Liberty** to the United States.
>   The French government shipped **her** in pieces to the United States.

✻ **Read each sentence. Underline the direct object.**

1. A team of engineers and laborers constructed the Statue of Liberty in France.

2. They packed the pieces of the statue into crates.

3. Workers loaded the crates on a ship bound for the United States.

4. In the United States, workers put the statue back together.

5. The Statue of Liberty greeted many immigrants.

6. Ships full of immigrants passed the statue before arriving in the United States.

7. She carries a torch in her upraised hand.

8. To immigrants, she represents hope and freedom.

✻ **Think of a direct object to complete each sentence. Write it on the line.**

9. Millions of immigrants gave up _____ to come to the United States.

10. Immigrants sought _____ in the United States.

11. They first visited _____.

12. The immigration agents at Ellis Island questioned the _____.

13. The immigration agents processed _____ slowly.

14. Many immigrants could not speak _____.

15. Starting over in a new country required _____.

16. They faced many _____.

17. Immigrants found _____ in big cities.

18. Big cities also offered _____.

Language: Usage and Practice 5, SV 1419027824

Name _____   Date _____

Pronouns

> - A **pronoun** is a word that takes the place of one or more nouns. Use pronouns to avoid repeating words.
> - A **singular pronoun** replaces a singular noun.
> - The words I, me, you, he, she, him, her, and it are singular pronouns.
> - A **plural pronoun** replaces a plural noun.
> - The words we, you, they, us, and them are plural pronouns.
>   EXAMPLES:
>   The man thought **he** should go to the store. (He takes the place of the man.)
>   The tourists searched for a place **they** could sleep that night. (They takes the place of the tourists.)

 Read each pair of sentences. Draw a line under the pronoun in the second sentence. Circle the word or words in the first sentence that the pronoun replaces.

1. Explorers came to Australia.

   They were amazed by the strange native animals and plants.

2. An animal the size of a greyhound lived there.

   It could leap like a grasshopper.

3. These animals are now known as kangaroos.

   Some of them can cover 27 feet in one jump.

4. Two interesting birds of Australia are emus and cassowaries.

   They cannot fly.

5. The early explorers told about the platypus.

   It is a mammal that lays eggs.

6. Scientists of the time did not believe the stories.

   They thought the stories were lies.

7. The coolabah of Western Australia is an interesting tree.

   It can survive frost as well as 120 degree heat.

8. The official flower of Western Australia is called the kangaroo paw.

   It looks like a paw and is even furry to the touch.

65

Name _____ Date _____

Agreement of Pronouns

- A pronoun is a word that takes the place of one or more nouns.
- Pronouns show number and gender. **Number** tells whether a pronoun is singular or plural. **Gender** tells whether the pronoun is masculine, feminine, or neuter.
- The **antecedent** of a pronoun is the noun or nouns to which the pronoun refers.
- A pronoun should agree with its antecedent in number and gender.

✳ **Write the pronoun that correctly completes the second sentence in each pair. Then circle the pronoun's antecedent in the first sentence.**

1. Mr. Les Harsten did an experiment with plants. _____ investigated with sound.

2. The man used two banana plants. He exposed _____ to the same amount of light.

3. Les also gave both plants the same amount of warmth and water. _____ did, however, change one thing.

4. One of the plants was exposed to a special sound for an hour a day. _____ was a high-pitched hum.

5. Les thought that sound might affect the plant. _____ was correct.

6. The plant exposed to the sound grew faster. In fact, _____ was 70 percent taller than the other plant.

7. All sounds won't work this way. Some of _____ can harm plants.

8. A recording of Harsten's sound is being sold. _____ is used by some plant growers.

9. Classical music works just as well with plants. _____ seem to thrive on it.

10. Hard rock music, however, does not work. _____ can stunt their growth.

11. You may want to play music for your plants. _____ may like it.

12. Some sounds help plants to grow. Do you think _____ would help you grow?

Name _____   Date _____

Subject and Object Pronouns

> • A **subject pronoun** is a pronoun that is used as the subject of a sentence.
> • <u>He</u>, <u>I</u>, <u>it</u>, <u>she</u>, <u>they</u>, <u>we</u>, and <u>you</u> are subject pronouns.
>   EXAMPLES: **She** helped Joe. **I** helped, too.
> • An **object pronoun** is a pronoun that is used in place of a noun that receives the action of the verb.
> • <u>Her</u>, <u>him</u>, <u>it</u>, <u>me</u>, <u>them</u>, <u>us</u>, and <u>you</u> are object pronouns.
>   EXAMPLES: Diane called **me**. I answered **her**.

 Circle the subject pronoun that could be used in place of the underlined subject.

1. <u>Jennifer</u> (Her, She) saw the bus nearing the corner.
2. <u>Chuck</u> (Him, He) ran down the street to stop the bus.
3. <u>The children</u> (Them, They) saw Jennifer from the bus windows.
4. <u>Angela</u> (Her, She) called to Ms. Thomas, the driver, to wait.
5. <u>The bus</u> (It, He) stopped just in time.
6. <u>Ms. Thomas</u> (Her, She) let Jennifer on the bus.
7. Then <u>Jennifer</u> (her, she) waved good-bye to Chuck.
8. <u>Jennifer</u> (Her, She) was glad the bus had waited for her.

 Circle the correct object pronoun that could be used in place of the underlined object.

9. Justin said, "Mark invited Willy and <u>Justin</u> (I, me) to his birthday party."
10. "He asked <u>Justin and Willy</u> (us, we) to be right on time," Willy said.
11. "Mark's friends are giving <u>Mark</u> (he, him) a special gift," Justin said. "They are giving him tickets to the baseball game."
12. "They bought <u>the tickets</u> (them, they) last week."
13. Willy asked, "Do you think Mark's friends bought <u>Mark, Willy, and Justin</u> (us, we) front-row seats?"
14. "Let's ask <u>Mark's friends</u> (them, they)," Justin answered.
15. "Front-row seats would be a treat for <u>Mark, Willy, and Justin</u> (us, we)," said Willy.

Name _____ Date _____

Possessive Pronouns

- A **possessive pronoun** is a pronoun that shows who or what owns something.
  - EXAMPLES: The shoes are **mine**. Those are **my** shoes.
- The possessive pronouns hers, mine, ours, theirs, and yours stand alone.
  - EXAMPLES: The dog is **mine**. This book is **yours**.
- The possessive pronouns her, its, my, our, their, and your must be used before nouns.
  - EXAMPLES: **Their** house is gray. **Her** cat is white.
- The pronoun his may be used either way.
  - EXAMPLES: That is **his** car. The car is **his**.

 Circle the possessive pronoun in parentheses that completes each sentence.

1. Carol lent me (her, hers) sweater.

2. I thought that (her, hers) was warmer than mine.

3. We often trade (our, ours) jackets and sweaters.

4. I hope I don't forget which are (her, hers) and which are (my, mine).

5. My cousin Pat and I have the same problem with (our, ours) bikes.

6. Both of (our, ours) are the same make and model.

7. The only difference is that (mine, my) handlebar grips are blue and (her, hers) are green.

8. What kind of dog is (your, yours)?

9. (Your, Yours) dog's ears are pointed.

10. (It, Its) tail is stubby.

 Complete each pair of sentences by writing the correct possessive pronoun.

11. Bill owns a beautiful horse named Sparky. _____ spots are brown and white.

12. Bill has taught the horse some tricks. In fact, _____ horse counts with its hoof.

13. Bill's sisters have horses, too. Bill is going to train them for _____ sisters.

14. I have a horse, too. _____ horse does not do tricks.

15. Bill's horse and my horse look alike. In fact, _____ horses could almost be twins!

Language: Usage and Practice 5, SV 1419027824

Reflexive Pronouns

- A **reflexive pronoun** refers to the subject of a sentence.
- The words <u>myself</u>, <u>yourself</u>, <u>himself</u>, <u>herself</u>, and <u>itself</u> are singular reflexive pronouns.
- <u>Ourselves</u>, <u>yourselves</u>, and <u>themselves</u> are plural reflexive pronouns.
    EXAMPLE: **Jackson** made **himself** eat the awful food.

✳ **Choose the reflexive pronoun in parentheses that correctly completes each sentence. Write the pronoun on the line.**

1. I will help _____ enjoy this vacation.
   (myself, ourselves)

2. Last year Daniel bought _____ a book about Australia.
   (himself, yourself)

3. The book concerned _____ with the history of the land.
   (itself, themselves)

4. Daniel's sister Erica made _____ read the book.
   (herself, ourselves)

5. "Daniel and Erica, teach _____ about Australia before our
   (yourself, yourselves)
   vacation," their mother said.

6. "That way, we can all enjoy _____ more," she continued.
   (myself, ourselves)

7. "Erica, buy _____ a good pair of walking shoes before the trip,"
   said her father. (yourself, yourselves)

8. Daniel and Erica imagined _____ having fun in Australia.
   (himself, themselves)

✳ **Write a reflexive pronoun on each line to complete the sentence.**

9. My sister and I will be treating _____ to a trip.

10. She still has to buy _____ a ticket.

11. I have bought _____ some new clothes for the trip.

12. Sharla, our travel agent, taught _____ the travel business.

13. Her partner, Monroe, talked _____ into learning it, too.

14. They want to earn _____ a good living.

Name _____   Date _____

Adjectives

- An **adjective** is a word that describes a noun or a pronoun.
  EXAMPLE: The field is filled with **colorful** flowers.
- Adjectives usually tell what kind, which one, or how many.
  EXAMPLES: **tall** trees   the **other** hat   **five** dollars

 In the sentences below, underline each adjective and circle the noun it describes. Some sentences may contain more than one adjective. Do not include a, an, or the.

1. The early Greeks thought a healthy body was important.

2. They believed that strong bodies meant healthy minds.

3. The Olympics began in Greece in the distant past.

4. The great god Zeus and the powerful Cronus both wanted to own Earth.

5. They battled on the high peaks of the beautiful mountains of Greece.

6. Zeus won the mighty struggle, and the first Olympics were held in the peaceful valley below Mount Olympus.

Expand the meaning of each sentence below by writing an adjective to describe each underlined noun.

7. The _____ runners from _____ nations lined up for the race.

8. Several _____ skaters competed for the _____ medal.

9. The _____ skiers sped down the _____ slopes.

10. We noticed the _____ colors of their _____ clothing against the _____ snow.

11. Hundreds of _____ fans greeted the _____ winners of each event.

12. As the _____ song of the winner's country was played, _____ tears streamed down her _____ face.

Fill in each blank with an adjective telling how many or which one.

13. _____ days of vacation

14. the _____ race

15. the _____ row of desks

16. _____ library books

Language: Usage and Practice 5, SV 1419027824

Name _____ Date _____

Proper Adjectives

- A **proper adjective** is formed from a proper noun.
- Capitalize each important word in a proper adjective.
  EXAMPLES: I like **Mexican** food.
  He sometimes reads a **European** newspaper.

 Underline the proper adjective in each sentence. On the line, write the proper noun from which it is formed. Use a dictionary if you need help.

1. Our modern Olympics come from an ancient Greek tradition.

   _____

2. The chariot races were often won by Spartan men.

   _____

3. An Athenian racer won three times in a row, starting in 536 B.C.

   _____

4. After 146 B.C., Roman athletes also competed in the games.

   _____

5. The 1988 Olympics took place in the Korean city of Seoul.

   _____

6. In 1976, a young Romanian girl, Nadia Comaneci, had seven perfect scores in gymnastics.

   _____

Complete each sentence by writing a proper adjective on the line. Form the proper adjective from the proper noun in parentheses.

7. Gertrude Ederle was the first woman to swim the _____ Channel.
   (England)

8. Sonja Henie was a famous _____ ice skater.
   (Norway)

9. Barbara Ann Scott was a _____ ice skater.
   (Canada)

10. Several _____ skaters have won awards in international
    (America)
    competition.

11. _____ teams always play good hockey.
    (Russia)

12. The _____ divers usually get high marks.
    (Japan)

Language: Usage and Practice 5, SV 1419027824

Name _____ Date _____

Predicate Adjectives

> - An adjective is a word that describes a noun.
> - A **predicate adjective** follows a linking verb such as <u>is</u>, <u>seems</u>, or <u>looks</u>.
> - When an adjective follows a linking verb, it can describe the subject of the sentence.
> - In some sentences, different adjectives in different positions describe the same noun or pronoun.
>   EXAMPLES:
>   Samuel is **young** and **bold**.
>   That snake looks **scary**.

 Circle the adjective following the linking verb in each sentence. Write the noun or pronoun the adjective describes.

1. These peanuts are crunchy. _____

2. They taste very salty. _____

3. The skin on the peanut is red. _____

4. Those pumpkin seeds look delicious. _____

5. Pumpkin seeds once seemed inedible. _____

6. They have grown popular lately. _____

7. Some quick snacks are healthful. _____

8. Green apples are sometimes sour. _____

9. This common fruit is crisp and juicy. _____

10. A crispy vegetable can be noisy if you eat it. _____

Write two adjectives to complete each sentence.

11. Bananas are _____

12. Pickles taste _____

13. Candy canes usually look _____

14. During the summer, watermelons become _____

15. With enough rain, pole beans will grow _____

Language: Usage and Practice 5, SV 1419027824

Name _____ Date _____

Articles and Demonstrative Adjectives

- The adjectives <u>a</u>, <u>an</u>, and <u>the</u> are called **articles**.
- Use <u>a</u> before a word that begins with a consonant sound.
- Use <u>an</u> before a word that begins with a vowel sound.
- Use <u>the</u> before a word that begins with a consonant or a vowel.
- <u>This</u>, <u>that</u>, <u>these</u>, and <u>those</u> are called **demonstrative adjectives**.
  EXAMPLES:
  Have you ever seen **an** owl?
  The owl is **a** nocturnal animal.
  That owl scared **those** people.

 Choose the adjective in parentheses that best completes each sentence. Write it on the line.

1. Many people have _____ strange idea about naturalists.
   (a, an)

2. _____ people regard naturalists as weird.
   (This, These)

3. They think naturalists wander around in forests, eating roots and berries along

   _____ way.
   (an, the)

4. Not all naturalists fit _____ description.
   (this, those)

5. You could be _____ naturalist yourself.
   (a, an)

6. You could learn _____ names of trees.
   (a, the)

7. You could also know when _____ chestnut is ready for roasting.
   (a, an)

8. You could tell whether _____ clay is better than that clay.
   (this, these)

9. You could figure out which way _____ wind is blowing.
   (the, these)

10. You could learn all _____ things easily.
    (this, these)

11. _____ good education is _____ key to success.
    (A, An)   (the, an)

12. You could become one of _____ weird naturalists, too!
    (that, those)

Language: Usage and Practice 5, SV 1419027824

Adjectives That Compare

> • Adjectives that compare two nouns end in <u>er</u>.
>   EXAMPLES: Jack is **taller** than Alonzo. Alonzo is **heavier**
>   than Jack.
> • Adjectives that compare more than two nouns end in <u>est</u>.
>   EXAMPLE: Monroe is the **tallest** and **heaviest** in the class.
> • Most longer adjectives use <u>more</u> and <u>most</u> to compare.
>   EXAMPLES: **more** beautiful, **most** beautiful

 Underline the correct form of the adjective.

1. Last year's science fair was the (bigger, biggest) one we have ever had.

2. For one thing, it had the (larger, largest) attendance ever.

3. Also, most students felt that the projects were (more interesting, most interesting) than last year's.

4. Of the two models of the solar system, Ray's was the (larger, largest).

5. However, Kaylee's model was (more accurate, most accurate) in scale.

6. The judges had a difficult task, but they gave the (higher, highest) rating to Kaylee's model.

7. Aaron's, Tina's, and Kyoto's projects on cameras drew the (bigger, biggest) crowds at the fair.

8. These projects were the (more popular, most popular) of all.

9. Tina's project had the (prettier, prettiest) display of photographs.

10. But Kyoto's showed the (greater, greatest) understanding of a camera's workings.

11. Aaron's project, however, was the (finer, finest) all-around project of the three.

12. One judge said, "This was the (harder, hardest) job I've ever had."

13. "Picking the (better, best) project was a challenge because all the projects were excellent," she said.

14. "I wonder if next year's contest will be (better, best) than this year's contest," said the judge.

15. "I hope my project next year will be the (more amazing, most amazing) one ever submitted," said Alex.

Language: Usage and Practice 5, SV 1419027824

Name _____   Date _____

Special Forms of Adjectives That Compare

- Some adjectives have special forms for comparing.
  EXAMPLES:
  Trixi has a **good** story.
  Chad's story is **better** than Trixi's.
  Leena's story is the **best** of all.

Adjective	Comparing Two Things	Comparing More Than Two Things
good	better	best
bad	worse	worst
little	less	least
much	more	most
many	more	most

❋ **Complete each sentence by choosing the correct form of the adjective in parentheses. Write it on the line.**

1. Hunger brought the Irish to America for a _____ life.
   (better, best)

2. About half of Ireland's farms had _____ than three acres of land.
   (less, least)

3. They had had the _____ potato crop in years.
   (worse, worst)

4. Each day _____ people were starving than the day before.
   (many, more)

5. Queen Victoria was told that the situation was becoming _____
   (worse, worst)
   every day.

6. She visited Ireland and said that she saw _____ ragged and
   (more, most)
   wretched people than she had seen anywhere else.

7. _____ Irish people chose Boston as their new home.
   (Many, Much)

8. Boston was the _____ convenient city for them because many ships
   (more, most)
   stopped there first.

Language: Usage and Practice 5, SV 1419027824

Adverbs

> • An **adverb** is a word that describes a verb. It tells how, when, where, or how often the action shown by a verb happens.
> • Many adverbs end in <u>ly</u>.
>   EXAMPLES: The bell rang **loudly**.   The bell rang **today**.
>   The bell rang **downstairs**.   The bell rang **often**.

 Circle each verb. Then underline each adverb that describes the verb. Next, write <u>how</u>, <u>when</u>, <u>where</u>, or <u>how often</u> to tell how the adverb describes the verb.

1. Rob and Jeff had (talked) <u>daily</u> about visiting the empty old house.   <u>how often</u>

2. They often walked by it on their way to school.   _____

3. But they seldom had time to stop.   _____

4. They suddenly decided that today was the day.   _____

5. So on the way home from school, they slipped quietly through the front gate.   _____

6. They crept carefully up the creaky front steps.   _____

7. Rob quietly opened the front door.   _____

8. Jeff then peered into the darkness of the front hall.   _____

9. A draft of wind instantly swept through the house.   _____

10. The back door banged loudly.   _____

11. Rob and Jeff ran swiftly out the front door and through the gate.   _____

12. They never returned to that empty old house.   _____

 Choose the correct adverb for each sentence. Write it on the line.

| finally   late   nervously   Suddenly |

13. Dean's plane was arriving _____.

14. Jancy kept glancing _____ at the clock in the airport.

15. _____ the gate lights flashed.

16. Dean's plane _____ had landed.

Language: Usage and Practice 5, SV 1419027824

Name _____ Date _____

Adverbs That Compare

- Add er when using short adverbs to compare two actions.
  EXAMPLE: Jasper ran **faster** than Showanda.
- Add est when using short adverbs to compare more than two actions.
  EXAMPLE: Jarrett ran **fastest** of all.
- Use more or most with longer adverbs and with adverbs that end
  in ly when comparing two or more than two actions.
  EXAMPLES:
  Tayor answered **more quickly** than Sharee.
  Antone answered **most quickly** of all.

✳ **Complete each sentence below by writing the correct form of
the adverb shown in parentheses.**

1. (close)   Amy lives _____ to Lake Hope than we do.

2. (early)   She usually arrives there _____ than we do.

3. (fast)   Amy says that I can row _____ than anyone else on
                 the lake.

4. (quickly)   But my cousin Jake can bait a hook _____ than I can.

5. (patiently)   Amy can wait _____ than Jake and I put together.

6. (carefully)   Jake and I are both careful, but Amy baits the hook _____.

7. (quietly)   Jake and I try to see who can sit _____.

8. (soon)   I usually break the silence _____ than Jake.

9. (skillfully) I'd have to admit that Amy fishes _____ of the three
                 of us.

10. (happily)   And no one I know welcomes us to her home _____
                 than she does.

11. (big)   Lake Hope is the _____ lake in our state.

12. (deep)   There is no lake _____ than Lake Hope.

13. (brave)   Only the _____ swimmers attempt to swim across
                 Lake Hope.

14. (strong)   Jake is a _____ swimmer than Amy, but he won't try
                 to swim across Lake Hope.

Language: Usage and Practice 5, SV 1419027824

Adverbs Before Adjectives and Other Adverbs

> - An adverb can be used to describe a verb.
> - An adverb can also be used to describe an adjective or another adverb.
>   EXAMPLES:
>   Macy did a **fairly** good job.
>   She thought **very** long about the question.

 Circle the adverb that describes the underlined adjective or adverb.

1. Reiko was sitting very <u>quietly</u> at her desk.

2. She felt extremely <u>interested</u> in the book.

3. The book was about carefully <u>planned</u> Japanese gardens.

4. Reiko quite <u>suddenly</u> decided to make one.

5. She knew her garden couldn't be too <u>big</u>.

6. She had a fairly <u>small</u> yard.

7. It was certainly <u>difficult</u> to choose a type of garden.

8. She considered the rather <u>difficult</u> job of making a garden with a pond.

9. Her yard was much <u>too</u> small for that.

 Draw an arrow from the underlined adverb to the adjective, other adverb, or verb it describes.

10. A teahouse garden is <u>particularly</u> charming.

11. It <u>gently</u> suggests an approach to a mountain temple.

12. The builder <u>skillfully</u> uses rocks and stones to suggest mountains and valleys.

13. Reiko didn't think this would work <u>effectively</u> in her yard.

14. She <u>finally</u> decided on a dry landscape garden.

15. A dry landscape garden is <u>much</u> less expensive than a teahouse garden to create.

16. Reiko's new garden looks <u>especially</u> beautiful.

17. Reiko is <u>particularly</u> proud of her garden gate.

18. The gate was <u>extremely</u> difficult to build.

19. Her design was <u>very</u> complicated.

20. It took <u>many</u> long hours to complete.

Language: Usage and Practice 5, SV 1419027824

Adjectives or Adverbs

- Remember that adjectives describe nouns or pronouns. Adjectives tell what kind, which one, or how many.
  EXAMPLES: **blue** sky   **this** year   **several** pages
- Remember that adverbs describe verbs, adjectives, or other adverbs. Adverbs tell how, when, where, or how often.
  EXAMPLES: Go **now**. Come **here**. Walk **very slowly**.

 In the sentences below, underline each adjective. Circle each adverb.

1. Three men were given licenses to hunt once on rugged Kodiak Island.

2. They had finally received permission to hunt the wild animals that live there.

3. Their purpose was different than the word "hunt" usually suggests.

4. The men were zoo hunters and would try to catch three bear cubs.

5. The young cubs would soon have a comfortable new home at a distant zoo.

6. When they reached the hilly island, the hopeful men quietly unpacked and then lay down for six hours of rest.

7. The next day, the men carefully scanned the rocky cliffs through powerful glasses.

8. They saw a huge brown bear with three cubs tumbling playfully around her.

9. The men spent two hours climbing quietly up to a point overlooking that ledge.

10. A large den could barely be seen in the rocks.

11. The wise men knew that bears never charge uphill.

12. However, the human scent immediately warned the watchful mother bear.

13. With a fierce roar, she walked heavily out of the cave and stared up at the men with her beady eyes.

14. One of the men tightly tied a red bandana and a dirty sock to a rope and threw the bundle down the slope.

15. The curious bear charged clumsily after it.

16. Quickly the men dropped to the wide ledge below.

17. But the clever cubs successfully hid from the men.

18. After many tries, the men finally gave up.

Name _____   Date _____

Prepositions

> - A **preposition** is a word that shows the relationship of a noun or a pronoun to another word in the sentence.
>   EXAMPLES: The cat **under** the tree is mine.
> - Some prepositions include in, down, to, by, of, with, for, and at.
> - A **prepositional phrase** is a group of words that begins with a preposition and ends with a noun or a pronoun.
>   EXAMPLES: **in** the house   **down** the street   **to** us

 Underline the prepositional phrase in each sentence below. Circle the preposition.

1. The box on the dining room table was wrapped.

2. A friend of Marta's was having a birthday.

3. Marta had been saving money for weeks so she could buy the present.

4. Now Marta was dressing in her bedroom.

5. Marta's little sister Tina toddled into the dining room.

6. She pulled the tablecloth, and the box fell to the floor.

7. Marta heard a thump and ran to the dining room.

8. Tina hid under the table.

9. The playful look on her face made Marta smile.

 Underline ten prepositional phrases in the paragraph below.

When I went into the store, I looked at coats. I needed a new one to wear during the winter. I left my old one on the bus. When I got on the bus, I noticed it was very hot. I removed my coat and put it under my seat. When I got off the bus, I forgot it. When I asked about it, I was told to look at the office. It was not in the office.

✳ **Give directions for a treasure hunt. Use the prepositional phrases below in your sentences.**

around the corner	near the school	under a rock	beneath the tree

_____

_____

_____

Name _____ Date _____

Prepositional Phrases

> • Remember that a prepositional phrase is made up of a preposition, the object of the preposition, and all the words in between.
>
> EXAMPLE: We started **in the morning** and worked **until sunset**.

 Underline each prepositional phrase. Circle the preposition.

1. Did you ever feel seasick in a car?

2. When you are seasick, you are not really sick from the sea.

3. You are sick from the motion of the waves.

4. In this same way, you can get sick in the back of a car.

5. Your sense of balance has been upset.

6. Deep inside your ears are semicircular canals.

7. These canals are filled with a fluid and are lined with special hairs.

8. These hairs pick up the sense of movement when you change position.

9. Usually, the fluid lies still in the bottom of the canals.

10. Quick, violent motions make the fluid move around the canals.

11. This can cause a sick feeling in your stomach.

 Add a prepositional phrase to each sentence. Write the new sentence on the line.

12. Lying down may help you feel better.

_____

13. There is less motion in the front seat, so you might move.

_____

_____

14. Reading can make motion sickness worse, so don't ever read.

_____

_____

Unit 3: Grammar and Usage
Language: Usage and Practice 5, SV 1419027824

Conjunctions

- A **conjunction** is a word that joins words or groups of words.
- Conjunctions may be used in several ways. The conjunction <u>and</u> is used to mean "together." The conjunction <u>but</u> is used to show contrast. The conjunction <u>or</u> is used to show choice.

    EXAMPLES:

    Patrick **and** the twins looked at their new home.

    His mother felt sad, **but** Patrick was excited.

    Did this old house hold mysteries **or** treasures?

 Complete each sentence, using the conjunction that has the meaning in parentheses.

1. The house looked bare _____ gloomy.
   (together)

2. The twins began to cry, _____ Patrick cheered them up.
   (contrast)

3. Patrick walked from room to room _____ looked for trapdoors.
   (together)

4. He did not find any trapdoors _____ mysterious stairways.
   (choice)

5. Patrick was disappointed, _____ his parents were glad.
   (contrast)

6. They did not want a house with ghosts _____ goblins in it.
   (choice)

7. Patrick told them there might be treasure _____ gold instead.
   (together)

8. His mother _____ father thought he was being silly.
   (together)

9. The treasure could be in the cellar _____ in the backyard.
   (choice)

10. He found a coin in the backyard near the cellar door, _____ he knew that he was right.
    (together)

11. People were coming to work on the house, _____ Patrick was afraid they would find the treasure first.
    (together)

12. His parents might think it was silly, _____ Patrick would not stop searching.
    (contrast)

Language: Usage and Practice 5, SV 1419027824

Interjections

- An **interjection** is a word or a group of words that expresses strong feeling.
  EXAMPLES:
  Help! My foot fell off!
  Wow! How did you do that?

 Circle the interjection in each item.

1. Gee! The baby is so tiny.

2. Wow! Her hands are so dainty.

3. She seems to be unhappy. Oh, dear!

4. Oh, my! What can we do to make her stop crying?

5. Good grief! That doesn't work.

6. Dad, where are you? Oops!

7. Great! Here comes Dad.

8. Alas! We cannot calm the baby. Can you help, Dad?

9. Of course! I'll show you what to do.

10. Gosh! That wasn't so hard.

Add an interjection to each exercise to express strong feeling. Punctuate correctly.

11. _____ She smiled at me!

12. _____ I knew she recognized me. I'm her brother, after all.

13. _____ I think the baby is going to sneeze.

14. She already did. _____

15. _____ I just dropped the rattle.

16. _____ I hope she doesn't start crying again.

17. _____ She's crying again.

18. _____ I can't stand all this noise!

19. _____ When will we get some peace and quiet around here?

20. That will happen after she leaves for college. _____

Language: Usage and Practice 5, SV 1419027824

Name _____   Date _____

Using *May/Can* and *Good/Well*

- <u>May</u> expresses permission.
    - EXAMPLE: **May** I go to town?
- <u>Can</u> expresses the ability to do something.
    - EXAMPLE: She **can** play well.
- <u>Good</u> is an adjective. It tells what kind.
    - EXAMPLE: My sister is a **good** cook.
- <u>Well</u> is an adverb. It tells how.
    - EXAMPLE: Did you do **well** today?

 Underline the correct word in parentheses to complete each sentence.

1. (Can, May) I use the pen on your desk, Sam?

2. Yes, you (can, may) use it, but I doubt that you (can, may) make it work, Sara.

3. Look, Sam! It's working (good, well) now.

4. That's (good, well). How did you make it work?

5. (Can, May) we have an early appointment, Doctor Morris?

6. Just a moment. I'll see whether I (can, may) arrange that.

7. Yes, I believe that will work out (good, well).

8. Thank you, doctor. That will be (good, well) for my schedule, too.

9. Juan, (can, may) we have these stacks of old magazines?

10. Of course you (can, may), Shelly.

11. Are you sure you (can, may) carry them, though?

12. I (can, may) help you if they are too heavy for you.

13. Thank you, Juan, but I'm sure that I (can, may) manage very (good, well).

14. That's a (good, well) money-making project you have. What is the money being used for?

15. We're raising money for new school band uniforms, and we're doing quite (good, well), too.

16. Ashley did a (good, well) job on her science project.

17. She did so (good, well) that she will take her project to the state fair this summer.

18. She will also bring a guest with her, and she has a (good, well) idea whom she will bring.

19. If Alan (can, may), he will do a project and go with her.

20. I think Alan will do (well, good) on his project.

Language: Usage and Practice 5, SV 1419027824

Using *Teach/Learn* and *Set/Sit*

- Teach means "to give instruction to others."
  EXAMPLE: Rosa will **teach** me to speak Spanish.
- Learn means "to get knowledge."
  EXAMPLE: I **will learn** to speak Spanish.
- Set means "to place something in a special position."
  EXAMPLE: Please **set** the books on the table.
- Sit means "to take a resting position."
  EXAMPLE: Please **sit** down and rest for a minute.

 Underline the correct word in parentheses to complete each sentence.

1. Andy: Who will (learn, teach) you to play the piano?

2. Pat: I hope to (learn, teach) from my sister, Sharla.

3. Andy: Wouldn't it be better to have Ms. Hill (learn, teach) you?

4. Pat: You were quite small when she began to (learn, teach) you.

5. Pat: Was it hard to (learn, teach) when you were so young?

6. Andy: Yes, but Ms. Hill let me (set, sit) on a high, round stool.

7. Andy: At home I would (set, sit) a thick book on the piano bench and (set, sit) on it.

8. Andy: Then I grew enough so that I could (set, sit) on the bench and still reach the keys.

9. April: Sharla asked Steve to (learn, teach) her how to drive.

10. April: She says it would make her nervous to have someone that she didn't know (learn, teach) her.

11. Tom: Are you going to go along and (set, sit) in the back seat?

12. April: I doubt that Sharla will want me to (set, sit) anywhere near when she is driving.

13. Scott: Amanda, I am going to (learn, teach) you a new skill.

14. Scott: I know you are old enough to (learn, teach) how to (set, sit) the table.

15. Scott: (Set, Sit) there, Amanda, so that you can watch me.

16. Scott: First I (set, sit) the plates in their places.

17. Scott: Then I put a glass at each place where someone will (set, sit).

18. Scott: Once I (learn, teach) you everything, you will be able to (set, sit) the table every night.

19. Amanda: Good! Let me try to (set, sit) it now.

20. Scott: When you are done, you can (set, sit) and rest.

Name _____   Date _____

Unit 3 Test

Darken the circle by the correct plural form of each underlined noun.

1. buggy
   - Ⓐ buggys
   - Ⓒ buggies
   - Ⓑ buggyes
   - Ⓓ buggeys

2. man
   - Ⓐ manes
   - Ⓒ mans
   - Ⓑ mens
   - Ⓓ men

3. box
   - Ⓐ boxs
   - Ⓒ boxies
   - Ⓑ boxes
   - Ⓓ boxss

4. shelf
   - Ⓐ shelves
   - Ⓒ shelvs
   - Ⓑ shelfs
   - Ⓓ shelfes

Darken the circle by the correct possessive form of each underlined noun.

5. Maria
   - Ⓐ Marias
   - Ⓒ Marias's
   - Ⓑ Marias'
   - Ⓓ Maria's

6. child
   - Ⓐ childs'
   - Ⓒ child's
   - Ⓑ childrens'
   - Ⓓ childs's

7. house
   - Ⓐ house's
   - Ⓒ hous's
   - Ⓑ houses'
   - Ⓓ housse

8. heroes
   - Ⓐ heroe's
   - Ⓒ hero'es
   - Ⓑ heroes'
   - Ⓓ heros'

Darken the circle by the correct answer to each question.

9. In which sentence is an action verb underlined?
   - Ⓐ We planned a picnic.
   - Ⓑ But each week it has rained.
   - Ⓒ Now the sun is out.
   - Ⓓ I hope it is sunny this weekend.

10. In which sentence is a helping verb underlined?
    - Ⓐ Mary has an Irish wolfhound.
    - Ⓑ I have seen it.
    - Ⓒ At first I was afraid.
    - Ⓓ But I find the dog is gentle.

Darken the circle by the sentence that contains a correct verb form of the verb tense shown.

11. past tense
    - Ⓐ We knew what had happened.
    - Ⓑ We known it would happen.
    - Ⓒ We know how things happen.
    - Ⓓ We will know when it happens.

12. future tense
    - Ⓐ I went to the seashore.
    - Ⓑ I will go to the seashore.
    - Ⓒ I have gone to the seashore.
    - Ⓓ I go to the seashore.

Language: Usage and Practice 5, SV 1419027824

Unit 3 Test, p. 2

Darken the circle by the verb that correctly completes each sentence.

13. Brendon and Gary _____ helping.

Ⓐ was   Ⓒ were

Ⓑ is   Ⓓ am

14. The truck _____ in the ditch.

Ⓐ were   Ⓒ is

Ⓑ am   Ⓓ are

15. Iris _____ the wrong turn.

Ⓐ took   Ⓒ has took

Ⓑ taken   Ⓓ take

16. She_____ three books.

Ⓐ write   Ⓒ had wrote

Ⓑ has wrote   Ⓓ has written

Darken the circle by the correct answer to each question.

17. In which sentence is the object pronoun underlined?

Ⓐ She waved hello to Mrs. Martelli.

Ⓑ They told him to go.

Ⓒ Randy's tie was too long.

Ⓓ Jerry and Ned spoke quietly.

18. In which sentence is the possessive pronoun underlined?

Ⓐ Its handle had broken.

Ⓑ No one had known about it before.

Ⓒ Watch out for them.

Ⓓ The people walked by slowly.

19. In which sentence is the subject pronoun underlined?

Ⓐ They invited us to a party.

Ⓑ Katy could not go to it.

Ⓒ Some dogs and cats like each other.

Ⓓ They are not friendly.

20. In which sentence is the adjective underlined?

Ⓐ The sky was brightly shining.

Ⓑ Clouds floated across the blue sky.

Ⓒ Patrick smiled happily at his brother.

Ⓓ Don't get too upset with them.

Darken the circle by the word that is used as a preposition in each sentence.

21. You didn't tell him to go into the cave.

Ⓐ You   Ⓒ into

Ⓑ him   Ⓓ cave

22. We had a great time at the beach.

Ⓐ we   Ⓒ time

Ⓑ at   Ⓓ the

Darken the circle by the sentence that is correct.

23. Ⓐ Can I have the mustard?

Ⓑ I did good today at work.

Ⓒ May I borrow that magazine?

Ⓓ Are you sure you may lift that?

24. Ⓐ Learn me how to play the piano.

Ⓑ Set it on the table.

Ⓒ That was a well book.

Ⓓ He sit his plate in the sink.

25. Ⓐ I hope you feel well today.

Ⓑ He learned her the first verse.

Ⓒ Todd may sing good.

Ⓓ I will teach how by myself.

26. Ⓐ It was well we went to see him.

Ⓑ The sun sit slowly in the west.

Ⓒ I will teach you to do that.

Ⓓ We can fix that very good.

    Language: Usage and Practice 5, SV 1419027824

Capitalizing First Words

> - Capitalize the first word of a sentence.
>   EXAMPLE: **M**any people have pen pals.
> - Capitalize the first word of a direct quotation.
>   EXAMPLE: Yung asked, "**W**here does your pen pal live?"

 Circle each letter that should be capitalized. Write the capital letter above it.

1. "have you met your pen pal?" I asked.

2. yung answered, "yes, he spent the holidays with me."

3. so I've invited my pen pal to visit me.

4. he hopes to arrive in my country next June.

5. i am making many plans for his visit.

6. we're going to hike in the mountains.

> - Capitalize the first word of every line of poetry.
>   EXAMPLE: **T**here was a monkey climbed up a tree;
>   **W**hen he fell down, then down fell he.
> - Capitalize the first, last, and all important words in the titles of
>   books, poems, stories, and songs.
>   EXAMPLE: Who wrote *Little House on the Prairie*?

 Circle each letter that should be capitalized. Write the capital letter above it.

7. there was an old woman

   lived under a hill,

   and if she's not gone,

   she lives there still.

8. if all the world were water,

   and all the water were ink,

   what should we do for bread and cheese?

   and what should we do for drink?

9. Have you read Longfellow's poem

   "the song of hiawatha"?

10. We are learning the song "down by

    the river."

11. If you're interested in ballooning, read

    up, up and away.

12. Mike wrote a story called "a balloon

    ride."

Language: Usage and Practice 5, SV 1419027824

Name _____ Date _____

Capitalizing Proper Nouns and Adjectives

- Capitalize all proper nouns.
  EXAMPLES: Main Street, Germany, Atlantic Ocean, Friday, Florida, Rocky Mountains, Halloween, December, Aunt Ann, Mom, Holmes School, James
- A proper adjective is an adjective that is made from a proper noun. Capitalize all proper adjectives.
  EXAMPLES: the English language, Italian dishes, French people, American tourists, the Australian cities

 Circle each letter that should be capitalized. Write the capital letter above it.

1. My friend larry had just returned from a world trip.

2. He brought gifts for everyone in my family, including my dog, chipper.

3. He gave my mother some delicate japanese dishes that he bought

   in tokyo, japan.

4. He gave my sister a scottish plaid kilt like the bagpipers wear

   in scotland.

5. My father really likes the hat larry got for him in london.

6. The hat reminds us of the kind sherlock holmes wore.

7. My gift was an african drum from mali in west africa.

8. larry told us how delicious the italian food was.

9. chipper's gift was a colorful, embroidered dog jacket from thailand.

 Write five sentences about a trip you would like to take. Use proper nouns and at least one proper adjective in the sentences.

10. _____

11. _____

12. _____

13. _____

14. _____

Capitalizing Titles and Abbreviations

> - Capitalize a person's title when it comes before a name.
>   EXAMPLES: Mayor Thomas, Governor Swanson
> - Capitalize abbreviations of titles.
>   EXAMPLES: Dr. Norris; Mr. and Mrs. J. B. Benton, Jr.; Ms. Harris; Mr. John F. Lynch, Sr.

 Circle each letter that should be capitalized. Write the capital letter above it.

1. We saw governor potter and senator williams in their offices.

2. They were discussing a national health problem with dr. laura bedford

    and mayor phillips.

3. We ate lunch with rev. barton and mr. james adams, jr.

4. They are part of a committee planning a welcome for prince charles

    of England, who will tour our state next month.

> - Capitalize abbreviations of days and months, parts of addresses, and titles of members of the armed forces. Also capitalize all letters in abbreviations for states.
>   EXAMPLES: Mon.; Sept.; 501 N. Elm St.; Capt. W. R. Russell; Chicago, IL

 Circle each letter that should be capitalized. Write the capital letter above it.

5. gen. david e. morgan

    6656 n. second ave.

    evanston, il 60202

6. valentine's day Exhibit

    at oak grove library

    mon.–fri., feb. 10–14

    101 e. madison st.

7. sgt. carlos m. martinez

    17 watling st.

    Shropshire SY7 0LW, england

8. maxwell school Field Day

    wed., apr. 30, 1:00

    Register mon.–tues., apr. 28–29

    mr. modica's office

Language: Usage and Practice 5, SV 1419027824

Using End Punctuation

- Use a **period** at the end of a declarative sentence.
  EXAMPLE: The lens is an important part of a camera.
- Use a **question mark** at the end of an interrogative sentence.
  EXAMPLE: Do you enjoy having your picture taken?

✳ **Add the correct end punctuation to each sentence below.**

1. Photography is an exciting hobby for many people
2. My friend Karen is one of those people
3. Have you ever gone on a vacation with a camera bug
4. Clay and I love Karen's photos
5. But getting those really good shots can be tiring
6. Can you imagine waiting in the hot desert sun while Karen gets just
   the right angle on a cactus
7. Or have you ever sat in the car while your friend waited for a grazing
   elk to turn its head
8. I don't need so much time when I take pictures
9. Of course, my pictures aren't always as good as Karen's

✳ **Add the correct end punctuation in the paragraphs below.**

   Have you ever wondered what it would be like to live as our country's
pioneers did___ You can visit log homes made to look like the original
cabins of pioneer days___ Then you can see how difficult life was for
the pioneers who helped our country grow___

   The cabins were small and roughly built___ Many cabins had just one
room___ Where was the kitchen___ Most of the cooking was done in the
large fireplace___ The fireplace also supplied the only heat___ Wasn't it
cold___ You can be sure the winter winds whistled between the logs___
And where did the pioneers sleep___ Most cabins had a ladder reaching
up to the bedroom loft___

   The furniture in the cabins was usually as roughly built as the cabins
themselves___ All the clothing was handmade by the family___ They ate
food grown and caught on their land___ Would you have liked to live in
those times___

Using End Punctuation, p. 2

> • Use a period at the end of an imperative sentence.
>   EXAMPLE: Please sign your name here.
> • Use an **exclamation point** at the end of an exclamatory sentence.
>   EXAMPLE: What a wonderful time we had at the show!

✼ **Add the correct end punctuation to each sentence below.**

10. A group of friends decided to go ice skating____

11. Terry asked, "Is Thursday OK with all of you____"

12. Carmen said, "It sounds great to me____"

13. They all agreed to meet at the lake____

14. Elaine said, "Wow, is it ever cold____"

15. "Get moving," said Leo. "You'll warm right up____"

16. They skated for several hours____

17. Terry asked, "Who's ready to sit close to a warm fire____"

18. Carmen said, "I thought you'd never ask____"

19. Suddenly she was hit by a snowball____

20. "Hey____"she shouted. "What's the big idea____"

21. Elaine laughed and said, "It's not that cold out____"

✼ **Add the correct end punctuation in the paragraphs below.**

  Have you ever seen pictures of northern Minnesota____ It is a region of many lakes____ My family once spent a week on Little Birch Lake____ What a sight it was____

  There were thousands of white birches reflected in the blue water____ The fishing was great____ Every day we caught large numbers of bass, and every night we cooked fresh fish for our dinner____

  The nearest town was Hackensack____ At the waterfront was a large statue of Diana Marie Kensack____ She is seated at the water's edge____ Her gaze is fixed on the horizon____ Do you know who she was____ Legends say that she was Paul Bunyan's sweetheart____ She is still waiting at the shore for him to come back to her____ Be sure to visit Diana when you are in Minnesota____

Direct Quotations and Dialogue

- Use a **direct quotation** to tell a speaker's exact words.
- Use **quotation marks (" ")** before and after the words a speaker says. Begin the first word a speaker says with a capital letter. Put end punctuation before the ending quotation marks.
- Begin a new paragraph each time the speaker changes.
- If the quotation is interrupted by other words, place quotation marks around the exact spoken words only.
  EXAMPLES: Mom asked, "Where have you been?"
  "I went to the store," Vince said. "Then I went to the library."

 Write quotation marks where they are needed in the following sentences.

1. Have you heard of the Nobel Peace Prize? asked Emi.

2. Yes. Mother Teresa and Nelson Mandela have won it, replied Jordan.

3. But do you know who Nobel was? Emi asked.

4. Jordan responded, No, I guess I don't.

5. He invented dynamite, stated Emi.

6. It seems weird, said Jordan, to name a peace prize for the inventor of dynamite.

7. In fact, Emi said, dynamite was once called Nobel's Safety Blasting Powder.

8. Nobel patented the blasting powder in 1867, Emi continued.

9. He did not want dynamite used for war, he said.

10. He added, Nobel once said that war is the horror of horrors and the greatest of all crimes.

11. How did the Nobel Prizes get started? asked Jordan.

12. Emi said, In his will, Nobel said that his money should be used to establish prizes in five areas: physics, chemistry, medicine, literature, and peace.

13. Sometimes a prize is shared by two or three people, he continued.

14. I'd like to know more about some of the winners, Jordan said.

15. Jimmy Carter, 39th President of the United States, won the Nobel Peace prize in 2002, replied Emi.

Language: Usage and Practice 5, SV 1419027824

Name _____ Date _____

Apostrophes and Colons

- Use an **apostrophe (')** to show that one or more letters have been left out in a contraction.
- To form a singular possessive noun, add an apostrophe and s to a singular noun.
- To form a plural possessive noun, add an apostrophe to a plural noun that ends in s.
- Add an apostrophe and s to plural nouns that do not end in s to show possession.
- Use a **colon (:)** between the hour and the minute in the time of day.
- Use a colon after the greeting in a business letter.

EXAMPLES: was not = wasn't   could not = couldn't
             Jane's father   the pig's tail
             guests' laughter   the maids' voices
             the children's adventure the men's story
             2:25 P.M.   5:13 A.M.
             Dear Ms. Parker: Dear Sir or Madam:

※ **Add apostrophes to the following items as needed.**

1. Uncle Chens problem was difficult to explain.

2. The childrens faces lit up when they saw him flying.

3. The boys smiles made Jane laugh.

4. "I cant stop laughing," Jane said.

5. "Wont you join us, Ms. Parker?" Jane asked.

6. Building a new home is many peoples dream.

7. It can also become a persons worst nightmare.

8. Cant you see that planning carefully is the key?

9. If you dont plan everything, somethings bound to go wrong.

10. Getting many opinions can help you decide whats best.

※ **Add colons to these items as needed.**

11. "It's only 3 30 in the afternoon," Michel said.

12. "We can stay until 6 00," Meri replied.

13. The movie starts at 7 15.

14. Dear Ms. Parson

    Your application for employment has been received.

Using Commas in Sentences

- Use a **comma** between words or word groups in a series.
  EXAMPLE: Food, medical supplies, blankets, and clothing were rushed to the flooded area.
- Use a comma to separate the parts of a compound sentence.
  EXAMPLE: Many homes were flooded, and the owners were taken to safety in boats.

 Add commas where needed in the sentences below.

1. The heavy rain caused flooding in Cedarville Taylorville Gardner and other towns along the Cedar River.

2. The flood washed away bridges roads and some small homes.

3. Our home had water in the basement and most of our neighbors' homes did, too.

4. We spent the night bailing mopping and worrying.

5. We put our washer and dryer up on blocks and then we helped Elaine.

6. Some of our shrubs flowers and small trees may have to be replaced.

7. Elaine's newly planted vegetable garden was washed away and the Smiths lost their shed.

8. The people in our neighborhood were very lucky and everyone agreed that the flood brought us closer together.

- Use a comma to separate a direct quotation from the rest of a sentence.
  EXAMPLES: "We're leaving now," said Ann.
  Ann said, "It's time to go."

Add commas where needed in the sentences below.

9. Sallee asked "Why did the rooster cross the road?"

10. "To get to the other side " answered Teri.

11. "That's really an old joke " Teri added.

12. Sallee asked "Do you know a newer one?"

13. Teri asked "What holds the moon up?"

14. "Moon beams " said Teri.

Using Commas in Sentences, p. 2

> • Use a comma to set off the name of a person who is addressed.
>   EXAMPLE: "Alan, can't you go with us?" asked Will.
> • Use a comma to set off words like <u>yes</u>, <u>no</u>, <u>well</u>, and <u>oh</u> when they begin a sentence.
>   EXAMPLE: "No, I have to visit my aunt," answered Alan.

 Add commas where needed in the sentences below.

15. "Melody and Tim would you like to go to the hockey game?" Marie asked.

16. "Oh yes!" Tim exclaimed.

17. "Marie I'd love to," called Melody.

18. "Well it's settled," said Marie.

19. "Ted did you go to the model show last night?" asked Sam.

20. "No I couldn't make it," answered Ted.

21. "Oh I was going to ask if Carlos won a prize," Sam said.

22. "Well I hope so," Ted said.

23. "Well then," Sam said, "let's call and ask him."

24. "Carlos did you win a prize last night?" Sam asked.

25. "Yes I did," replied Carlos.

26. "Oh what did you win?" asked Sam.

27. "Well you'd never guess," answered Carlos.

28. "Carlos don't keep us guessing," said Sam.

29. "Well you know my model was of a helicopter. My prize was a ride in a helicopter!" exclaimed Carlos.

 Pretend that you and your friends are planning an outing. Write a conversation that might take place between you and your friends. Use the names of the persons being addressed. In some sentences, use yes, no, oh, or well. Punctuate your sentences correctly.

_____

_____

_____

_____

_____

Language: Usage and Practice 5, SV 1419027824

Unit 4 Test

Darken the circle by the word in each sentence that should be capitalized.

1. we will take our vacation to the mountains in June.
   - Ⓐ we
   - Ⓑ our
   - Ⓒ vacation
   - Ⓓ mountains

2. Have you read *Treasure island,* the exciting adventure story?
   - Ⓐ read
   - Ⓑ island
   - Ⓒ adventure
   - Ⓓ story

3. Your friend judy likes the books that author has written.
   - Ⓐ friend
   - Ⓑ judy
   - Ⓒ books
   - Ⓓ author

4. My friend likes to read poetry written by japanese poets.
   - Ⓐ friend
   - Ⓑ poetry
   - Ⓒ japanese
   - Ⓓ poets

5. Have you read governor Palmer's book about his life?
   - Ⓐ you
   - Ⓑ governor
   - Ⓒ book
   - Ⓓ life

6. The english language is spoken in many countries.
   - Ⓐ english
   - Ⓑ language
   - Ⓒ spoken
   - Ⓓ countries

7. The letter was mailed yesterday to 478 s. Baker Street.
   - Ⓐ letter
   - Ⓑ s.
   - Ⓒ mailed
   - Ⓓ yesterday

8. When did you see mrs. Webb and her children?
   - Ⓐ you
   - Ⓑ mrs.
   - Ⓒ her
   - Ⓓ children

9. sara and I are going to the museum tomorrow.
   - Ⓐ sara
   - Ⓑ going
   - Ⓒ museum
   - Ⓓ tomorrow

10. We want to see the Franklin d. Roosevelt exhibit.
    - Ⓐ want
    - Ⓑ see
    - Ⓒ d.
    - Ⓓ exhibit

Darken the circle by the sentence in which commas are used correctly.

11.
- Ⓐ I served fruit milk and cheese.
- Ⓑ Julia Billy and Mark, like fruit.
- Ⓒ Julia had apples, bananas, and milk.
- Ⓓ Sue had cheese, grapes, and, milk.

12.
- Ⓐ Jan, and I heard about a new show.
- Ⓑ Mary called and, asked us to go.
- Ⓒ I'd like to go today, but Jan can't.
- Ⓓ We want to wait and, go together.

13.
- Ⓐ Bears, and wolves live in the wild.
- Ⓑ Wildlife today, is in danger.
- Ⓒ Hunters shoot, many wild animals.
- Ⓓ Bears, wolves, and other animals should be saved.

14.
- Ⓐ It rained hard, and then it stopped.
- Ⓑ The clouds, and fog, went away.
- Ⓒ Sunshine dried the grass, and sidewalks.
- Ⓓ It was too dark, to go for a walk.

In which sentence are quotation marks used correctly?
Darken the circle by your choice.

15. (A) "We're leaving now, said Melinda."
    (B) "Do we have to go?" Juan asked.
    (C) Yes, we do," Melinda answered.
    (D) "You will have a good time.

16. (A) "Hello," said Jim. How are you?"
    (B) "I'm fine, answered Joe."
    (C) "Joe, said Jim, are you ready"?
    (D) "No," said Joe, "I'm not."

17. (A) "What is the point? asked Bill.
    (B) "Well," said Paula, I don't know."
    (C) "Who can tell us?" asked Bill.
    (D) "Paula said, Let's ask Michael."

18. (A) Don't eat that!" cried Alice.
    (B) "You scared me to death, said Luis.
    (C) "Don't you know that's for dinner?
    (D) "No, I thought it was for me!"

In which sentence is end punctuation used correctly?
Darken the circle by your choice.

19. (A) I remember our trip to Montana?
    (B) Jerome had just learned to drive.
    (C) Wasn't he a good driver.
    (D) What a great time we had?

20. (A) What a game we just saw?
    (B) What was so good about it.
    (C) We won!
    (D) Shall we play tomorrow.

21. (A) May I ask you a question.
    (B) Go ahead?
    (C) Why did you move here!
    (D) I wanted to see a new place.

22. (A) Aren't you happy now.
    (B) Yes, I am?
    (C) This is fantastic!
    (D) Don't you just want me to try.

In which sentence are apostrophes used correctly?
Darken the circle by your choice.

23. (A) I cant' believe you said that.
    (B) We've been over this before.
    (C) Why do'nt you understand?
    (D) Il'I explain it again.

24. (A) They're on the way now.
    (B) Its' been a long time.
    (C) Wev'e missed seeing them.
    (D) I'm sure theyv'e been busy.

25. (A) Hed' better not do that.
    (B) And whol'l tell him?
    (C) I'll do it.
    (D) Okay, that way hes' safe.

26. (A) Taras' house is beautiful.
    (B) It was her husband's plan.
    (C) Their houses' front porch is huge.
    (D) Their childrens' rooms are, too.

Language: Usage and Practice 5, SV 1419027824

Writing Sentences

> - Every sentence has a base. The **sentence base** is made up of a simple subject and a simple predicate.
>   EXAMPLE: <u>Men</u> **stared**.
> - Add other words to the sentence base to expand the meaning of the sentence.
>   EXAMPLE: **The bewildered** men stared **in amazement at the mysterious light**.

 Expand the meaning of each sentence base below. Add adjectives, adverbs, and/or prepositional phrases. Write your expanded sentence.

1. (Plane flew.) _____

2. (Creatures ran.) _____

3. (Dogs played.) _____

4. (Police chased.) _____

5. (Boys discovered.) _____

Imagine two different scenes for each sentence base below. Write an expanded sentence to describe each scene you imagine.

6. (Children explored.) **a.** _____

   b. _____

7. (Fire was set.) **a.** _____

   b. _____

8. (Crowd roared.) **a.** _____

   b. _____

9. (Wind blew.) **a.** _____

   b. _____

10. (Friend sent.) **a.** _____

    b. _____

11. (Actor was dressed.) **a.** _____

    b. _____

Language: Usage and Practice 5, SV 1419027824

Paragraphs

- A **paragraph** is a group of sentences that tells about one main idea.
- The first line of a paragraph is indented. This means the first word is moved in a little from the left margin.
- The **topic sentence** expresses the main idea of the paragraph. It tells what all the other sentences in the paragraph are about. The topic sentence is often the first sentence in a paragraph.
- The other sentences in a paragraph are **detail sentences**. Detail sentences add information about the topic sentence. They help the audience understand more about the main idea.

EXAMPLE:

Optical illusions occur when your eyes and brain give you the wrong idea about the way something looks. In one kind of optical illusion, the brain compares the images you see to images in your memory. Then your brain makes the wrong interpretation about the new image. Another optical illusion takes place when the brain cannot choose between equally possible interpretations. In yet another, the brain works perfectly well. However, the bending of light through the atmosphere creates mirages that fool your eyes.

Complete this chart with information from the example paragraph.

Main Idea: _____

_____

Detail: _____

_____

Detail: _____

_____

Detail: _____

Writing Topic Sentences (Main Idea)

> • A topic sentence is a sentence that states the main idea of a paragraph.
>   EXAMPLE: **Many of the best things in life are free.** The sun and the moon give their light without charge. A true friend can't be bought. The beauty of the clouds in a blue sky is there for all to enjoy.

✳ **Write a topic sentence for each of the paragraphs below.**

1. The summer had been extremely hot and dry. Many brush fires had broken out. People were told not to water their lawns or wash their cars. People responded by using less water and being careful about how they used water. Everyone realized the new rules were in the best interest of everyone.

    Topic Sentence: _____

2. Neena read everything she could find about nursing. She spent hours in the library learning about first aid. When the call came for summer volunteers at the hospital, she was the first to sign up. She was determined to prepare herself as best she could for what she hoped would be her career.

    Topic Sentence: _____

3. There are many parks to enjoy. Museums and aquariums have interesting exhibits. Large stores and malls have a great selection of things to buy. Many large cities also have major sports teams to watch.

    Topic Sentence: _____

✳ **Choose one of the topics below. Write a topic sentence for it. Then write a paragraph of about fifty words in which you develop the topic.**

at least 5-6 sentences

The Most Useful Invention	My Favorite Holiday
A Frightening Experience	A Place I Want to Visit

_____

_____

_____

_____

_____

_____

_____

Name _____ Date _____

Writing Supporting Details

- Sentences that contain supporting details develop the topic sentence of a paragraph.
- The details may be facts, examples, or reasons.

 Read the topic sentence below. Then read the numbered sentences. Underline the four sentences that contain details that support the topic sentence.

Topic Sentence: Automobile seat belts save lives.

1. The first seat belts didn't have shoulder straps.
2. A seat belt helps keep a front-seat passenger from going through the windshield.
3. A passenger who doesn't fasten his or her seat belt may be hurt if the car is in an accident.
4. Seat belts protect small children from falls and bumps while riding in the back seat.
5. Some cars today have automatic seat belts.
6. Studies on the number of lives saved prove the value of wearing seat belts.

 Underline the correct word to complete the sentence.

7. The supporting details in the sentences above were (facts, examples, reasons).

Choose one of the topic sentences. Write it on the first line. Then write three sentences that contain supporting details. The details may be facts, examples, or reasons.

a. Having a pet is a lot of work.
b. A large (or small) family has advantages.
c. My vacation (in the mountains, at camp, on the seashore, or other place) was fun.
d. Every student should have an allowance.

_____

_____

_____

_____

Complete the sentence below by writing the word facts, examples, or reasons.

8. The supporting details in my paragraph were _____.

Language: Usage and Practice 5, SV 1419027824

Name _____ Date _____

Comparing and Contrasting

- **Comparing** two objects, persons, or ideas shows the likenesses between them. Comparing expresses a thought in a colorful, interesting way.
  - EXAMPLE: Walking lets the walker be as free as a bird that has flown from its cage.
- **Contrasting** two objects, persons, or ideas shows the differences between them. Contrasting can also express a thought in a colorful, interesting way.
  - EXAMPLE: Baby Rachel's morning mood is one of sunshine, rainbows, and laughter. Her naptime mood, however, suggests gathering clouds.

 Read each topic sentence and the pair of sentences that follow. Underline the sentence that expresses a supporting detail in a colorful, interesting way.

1. **Topic Sentence:** Having the flu is no fun.
   a. Pat was tired of being in bed with the flu.
   b. After a week in bed with the flu, Pat felt like her pet hamster, Hamby, spinning his wheel in his cage.

2. **Topic Sentence:** Koalas aren't all they seem to be.
   a. A koala is cute but unfriendly.
   b. A koala looks like a cuddly teddy bear, but it is about as friendly as a grizzly bear.

 Rewrite each sentence below in a more colorful, interesting way. Use comparison or contrast.

3. A mosquito bite is itchy.

   _____

4. Taking a bus to a museum is fun.

   _____

5. Dogs are friendlier than cats.

   _____

6. Reading is a good way to spend your free time.

   _____

7. Stealing a base makes baseball exciting.

   _____

Name _____   Date _____

Using Location

> • Supporting details can be arranged in order of location.
>   EXAMPLE: The sofa was **on the long wall to your right**.
>   A table sat **at each end** of the sofa.

 In the paragraph below, underline the words that show location.

    I stood watching. <u>Below me</u> was the ball field. Across the street from the ball field, men were building an apartment house. Cement trucks were lined up along the street. They were delivering concrete for the basement walls of the apartment house. A kindergarten class was playing baseball on the ball field. The wise teacher told the class to move away from the street.

 Choose one of the scenes or objects below. Write a topic sentence about it. Then write a paragraph of at least five sentences describing the scene or object. Use words such as <u>above</u>, <u>ahead</u>, <u>around</u>, <u>behind</u>, <u>next to</u>, <u>on top of</u>, and <u>under</u> to show location. Then underline the words you used to show location.

    Scenes: your street, your home, a garden
    Objects: your bicycle, a car, your favorite book

_____

_____

_____

_____

_____

_____

_____

_____

_____

_____

_____

Name _____ Date _____

Topic and Audience

- The **topic** of a paragraph should be something the writer is interested in or familiar with.
  EXAMPLES: school, animals, science, sports, hobbies
- The **title** should be based on the topic.
- The **audience** is the person or people who will read what is written.
  EXAMPLES: classmates, readers of the class newspaper, family members

 Suppose that the topic chosen is <u>sports</u>. Underline the sports topic below that you would most like to write about.

1. Is winning the most important thing in sports?

2. There are many reasons why tennis (or baseball, or swimming, or _____) is my favorite sport.

3. Sports can be an enjoyable family activity.

 Think about the topic you underlined above. Underline the audience below that you would like to write for.

4. your family

5. a coach

6. your best friend

Write a paragraph of about seventy words, using the sentence you underlined above as your topic sentence. Write a title for your paragraph. Direct your paragraph to the audience you chose above.

_____

_____

_____

_____

_____

_____

_____

_____

Name _____ Date _____

Clustering

- **Clustering** uses a special drawing that shows how ideas relate to one main topic.
- That topic is written in a center shape. Other shapes contain the ideas.
- Lines show how the ideas are connected to the main topic.
  EXAMPLE:

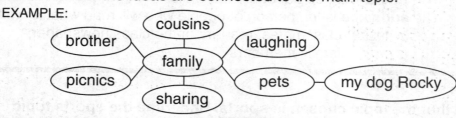

Topic Sentence: My family is wonderful.

 Complete each cluster below by writing words that the topic makes you think of. You may add additional shapes and connecting lines. Then write a topic sentence using each topic.

1.

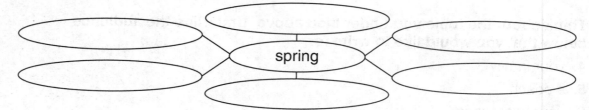

Topic Sentence: _____

2.

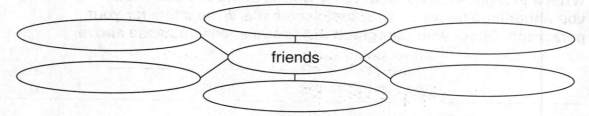

Topic Sentence: _____

 Choose one of the topics above. Write it on the title line below. Then write your topic sentence for that topic. Complete the paragraph.

_____

_____

_____

_____

_____

Name _____   Date _____

A Descriptive Paragraph

- A **descriptive paragraph** describes something.
- It is made colorful and interesting through the use of details.
  EXAMPLE: A **thick coating** of dust covered everything in the **old abandoned** house.

 Read the descriptive paragraph below. Then answer the question.

In my neighborhood, there is a small grocery store just a block from my house. A couple, Mr. and Mrs. Aggens, are the owners. I always hope that Mrs. Aggens will wait on me. She is friendly and full of smiles. She always gives me extra-large scoops of ice cream. She doesn't hurry me when I can't decide whether to spend my money on apples or fruit bars. After I make my purchase, I like to stay, smell the freshly ground coffee, and talk to Mrs. Aggens.

1. What kind of person is Mrs. Aggens? Circle the words that describe her.

   crabby, patient, impatient, kind, stingy, generous

 Read the paragraph below about the same store.

In my neighborhood, there is a store near our house. The owners are a husband and wife. The wife is patient, generous, and friendly. Near the door is a fruit counter and an ice cream counter. I often shop there.

2. List at least five details that are missing from this paragraph. _____

   _____

   _____

3. What is the result of leaving out these details? _____

   _____

 Write a descriptive paragraph about a place you visit often. Use details to make your paragraph colorful and interesting.

   _____

   _____

   _____

   _____

   _____

Language: Usage and Practice 5, SV 1419027824

Name _____ Date _____

Writing a Descriptive Paragraph

- Writers use descriptive words that tell how something looks, feels, smells, tastes, or sounds.
    EXAMPLE: The **shady** forest was dressed in the **soft greens** and **pale yellows** of early spring.
- Writers use verbs that tell exactly what someone is doing or how someone moves.
    EXAMPLE: Richard **tramped** across the newly mopped kitchen floor.

 Read the paragraph below and answer the questions that follow.

   Jody stood silently at the rickety gate of Harry's weathered old ranch house. The crooked gate hung on only its top hinge. The house, which had never known a paintbrush, seemed to have become gray with age. A gentle breeze rippled the tall grass and filled Jody's nostrils with the sugary smell of sweet peas. Jody turned. Yes, there were those lovely white, pastel pink, and lavender blooms. But everything else had faded with age.

1. What words tell how the ranch house looked? _____

   How the gate looked? _____

2. What word tells how the breeze felt? _____

   How the grass looked? _____ How it moved? _____

   How the sweet peas smelled? _____ How they looked? _____

 Choose a familiar place to write about in a descriptive paragraph. Write a topic sentence to begin the paragraph. Think about how the place looks, the sounds you might hear there, the smells you might smell there, how it feels to be there, and the things you might taste there. Write descriptive sentences that tell about these things to complete your paragraph.

_____

_____

_____

_____

_____

_____

_____

Name _____   Date _____

Revising and Proofreading

- **Revising** gives you a chance to rethink and review what you have written and to improve your writing.
- Revise by adding words and information, by deleting unneeded words and information, and by moving words, sentences, and paragraphs around.
- **Proofreading** involves checking spelling, punctuation, grammar, and capitalization.
- Use proofreader's marks to show changes needed.

Proofreader's Marks

Capitalize.

Add a period.

Correct spelling.

Make a small letter.

Add something.

Indent for new paragraph.

Add a comma.

Take something out.

Move something.

Rewrite the paragraphs below. Correct the errors by using the proofreader's marks.

during the history of Earth there have been several ice ages these were times when giant sheets of ice spred across many parts of earth. People think that almost one third of the land was covered by these hug sheets of ice.

The last ice age frozed so so much ocean water that the level of the oceans dropped. then lots of land apeared that usually lay underwater When the tempeture began to warm up the ice sheets melted. The Ocean levels rose again.

_____

_____

_____

_____

_____

_____

Unit 5: Composition
Language: Usage and Practice 5, SV 1419027824

Name _____   Date _____

Unit 5 Test

Read the paragraph. Then darken the circle by the correct answer to each question.

Most American newspapers have a separate section for sports news. Many people even read the sports section first. Sports magazines are also very popular. Television and radio cover sporting events almost daily. Crowds fill our stadiums and parks. Many fans stand for hours to buy tickets. Others buy season tickets so they can watch their favorite team often.

1. Which sentence could best be a topic sentence for the paragraph above?
   Ⓐ My favorite sport is baseball.
   Ⓑ *Sports Illustrated* magazine covers many different sports.
   Ⓒ Americans show a tremendous interest in sports.
   Ⓓ Many Americans are athletic.

2. Which sentence would <u>not</u> be a supporting detail for this paragraph?
   Ⓐ Some American magazines cover just one sport, in detail.
   Ⓑ Many Americans watch the Olympics.
   Ⓒ I read a good magazine last night.
   Ⓓ Many people collect athletes' autographs.

3. What is the purpose of a topic sentence?
   Ⓐ to give an opinion
   Ⓑ to state the main idea of a paragraph
   Ⓒ to support the main idea of a paragraph
   Ⓓ to introduce the writer

4. Which audience would <u>not</u> be interested in the paragraph above?
   Ⓐ coaches
   Ⓑ teenagers
   Ⓒ babies
   Ⓓ adults

Darken the circle by the correct answer to each question.

5. Which is a descriptive word?
   Ⓐ and   Ⓒ crabby
   Ⓑ so   Ⓓ is

6. Which sentence uses comparison to describe?
   Ⓐ I like to play baseball.
   Ⓑ My brother is a very good swimmer.
   Ⓒ Hang gliding makes people feel as free as a bird.
   Ⓓ Our team won the relay race.

7. What is a title based on?
   Ⓐ topic   Ⓒ location
   Ⓑ contrast   Ⓓ comparison

8. Which words would be used often in a paragraph using location?
   Ⓐ taste, smell, sound
   Ⓑ itchy, gentle, harsh
   Ⓒ swim, dive, pool
   Ⓓ above, behind, next to

Name _____ Date _____

Read the paragraph. Then darken the circle by the correct answer to each question.

Language is a set of written or spoken symbols used to communicate. It is a powerful tool. Language lets parents teach their children. It gives people a way to share what they know and what they do. Language allows people to write down their experiences and feelings. These written records let people pass on their skills and knowledge.

9. Which sentence could best be a topic sentence for the paragraph above?
- Ⓐ People from different countries speak different languages.
- Ⓑ People use language to communicate with each other.
- Ⓒ People can speak with words and with hand motions.
- Ⓓ Reading teaches people what others know.

10. Which sentence would be a supporting detail for this paragraph?
- Ⓐ Working with tools is another skill people have.
- Ⓑ Animals do not have a common language.
- Ⓒ Knowledge is what people know.
- Ⓓ All humans talk to each other in some way.

Darken the circle by the correct answer to each question.

11. Which proofreader's mark means to add something?
- Ⓐ ∧
- Ⓑ ⊙
- Ⓒ ℮
- Ⓓ ⤳

12. Which proofreader's mark means to move something?
- Ⓐ ⊙
- Ⓑ ℮
- Ⓒ ⤳
- Ⓓ ¶

13. Which proofreader's mark means to take something out?
- Ⓐ ⤳
- Ⓑ ⊙
- Ⓒ ¶
- Ⓓ ℮

14. Which proofreader's mark means to capitalize?
- Ⓐ /
- Ⓑ ⊙
- Ⓒ ≡
- Ⓓ ¶

15. Which proofreader's mark means to add a period?
- Ⓐ ∧
- Ⓑ ⊙
- Ⓒ ℮
- Ⓓ /

16. Which proofreader's mark means to make a small letter?
- Ⓐ ⋏
- Ⓑ /
- Ⓒ ≡
- Ⓓ ⊙

Name _____ Date _____

Following Directions

- When following written directions, it is important to read each step carefully.
- Be sure you have completed one step before going on to the next step.

 Read the recipe below. Then answer the questions that follow it.

Peanut Butter Balls

$\frac{1}{2}$ cup wheat germ $\frac{1}{2}$ cup powdered milk

$\frac{1}{2}$ cup sunflower seeds $\frac{1}{2}$ cup honey

$\frac{1}{2}$ cup peanut butter $\frac{1}{2}$ cup sesame seeds (if desired)

a. Spread wheat germ and sunflower seeds on a cookie sheet. Bake at 350° for 15 minutes, stirring every 5 minutes.

b. Place toasted wheat germ and sunflower seeds in a bowl.

c. Add all other ingredients except sesame seeds. Mix well.

d. Form into balls, using 1 teaspoonful of dough for each ball.

e. Roll balls in sesame seeds. (This step is not necessary.)

f. Chill for 3 hours.

g. Serve as a tasty, good-for-you snack or dessert.

1. What is the recipe for? _____

2. What kitchen utensils are needed? _____

3. What quantity of each ingredient is needed? _____

4. What ingredients are used in step a? _____

5. What should the oven temperature be? _____

6. How long should the wheat germ and sunflower seeds

   be baked? _____

7. How often should you stir the wheat germ and sunflower seeds

   while they are baking? _____

8. How much dough is needed to form each ball? _____

9. How long should the peanut butter balls be chilled before eating?

   _____

10. Which ingredient may be left out? _____

Name _____ Date _____

Alphabetical Order

- **Alphabetical order** is used in many kinds of listings.
  EXAMPLE: Miss Clark's class list: Adams, Coss, Edwards, Gutierrez, Lee, Ortega, Shapiro, Turner

 Complete each sentence below.

1. The letter <u>n</u> comes after _____ and before _____.

2. The letters between <u>s</u> and <u>w</u> are _____.

- Entries in a dictionary or an encyclopedia appear in alphabetical order, according to their first letters, second letters, third letters, and so on.
  EXAMPLE: wave, wax, web, weed, wish, wisp

 Number the words in each group in alphabetical order.

    3   4   2   1

3. whale, where, weary, water

4. school, second, safety, sailor

5. earth, ease, each, earn

6. recess, rain, ring, rose

 Number the encyclopedia entries in each column in alphabetical order.

7. _____ Bell, Alexander Graham

    _____ Berlin

    _____ Bear

8. _____ Panda

    _____ Pago Pago

    _____ Panama Canal

- Names in a telephone book are listed in alphabetical order, according to last names.
- When several people have the same last name, their names are arranged in alphabetical order, according to first names.
  EXAMPLE: Barnes, John; Barnes, William; Barton, Clyde; Barwin, James D.

 Copy the names in the order you would find them in a telephone book.

9. T. C. Caskey _____

    Louis J. Caskey _____

    Cindy Lyons _____

    Paul Lyndale _____

Unit 6: Study Skills
Language: Usage and Practice 5, SV 1419027824

Name _____ Date _____

Dictionary: Guide Words

> - **Guide words** are words that appear at the top of each page in a dictionary.
> - They show the first and last entry words on the page. Guide words tell whether an entry word is listed on that page.
>   EXAMPLE: **beets/beyond**
>   The word begin will appear on the page.
>   The word bid will not.

✳ **Read each pair of guide words and the list of entry words below. Put a check in front of each entry word that would appear on the page.**

1. blade/bluff

_____ blur	_____ blast
_____ blink	_____ black
_____ blame	_____ blaze
_____ blossom	_____ blunder
_____ blush	_____ blouse

2. intend/island

_____ into	_____ invent
_____ instrument	_____ isn't
_____ introduce	_____ irrigate
_____ iron	_____ itch
_____ inward	_____ invite

✳ **Read each pair of guide words and the list of entry words below. Circle only the entry words that would appear on the page. Then write those words in the order in which they would appear in the dictionary.**

3. meal/minister

meanwhile _____

melody _____

meadow _____

mention _____

mischief _____

4. product/provide

professor _____

propeller _____

proceed _____

program _____

protest _____

5. rear/rescue

recess _____

realize _____

recognize _____

reckon _____

receive _____

6. miserable/mitten

mist _____

mischief _____

miss _____

mite _____

mixture _____

Unit 6: Study Skills
Language: Usage and Practice 5, SV 1419027824

Name _____   Date _____

Dictionary: Syllables

> - A **syllable** is each part of a word that is pronounced at one time.
> - Dictionary entry words are divided into syllables to show how to divide a word at the end of a writing line.
> - Put a **hyphen (-)** between syllables when dividing a word.
>   EXAMPLE: a-wak-en

 Find each word in a dictionary. Write the word, placing a hyphen between syllables.

1. chemical _____
2. gasoline _____
3. decree _____
4. marvelous _____
5. disappear _____
6. chimney _____
7. continental _____
8. miserable _____
9. generally _____
10. glacier _____
11. arithmetic _____
12. exercise _____
13. hospital _____
14. problem _____
15. window _____
16. language _____
17. agriculture _____
18. parakeet _____
19. beginning _____
20. simple _____

21. determine _____
22. musician _____
23. salary _____
24. cheetah _____
25. interrupt _____
26. dentist _____
27. recognize _____
28. rascal _____
29. innocent _____
30. educate _____
31. achievement _____
32. darling _____
33. homestead _____
34. calendar _____
35. missionary _____
36. farewell _____
37. aluminum _____
38. bacteria _____
39. program _____
40. banana _____

Unit 6: Study Skills
Language: Usage and Practice 5, SV 1419027824

Name _____   Date _____

Using an Encyclopedia

- An **encyclopedia** is a reference book that has articles on many different subjects.
- The articles are arranged in alphabetical order in different books, called **volumes**. Each volume is marked to show which subjects are inside.
- **Guide words** are used to show the first subject on each page.
- **Cross-references** to related subjects are listed at the end of most articles, so that the reader can get more information on that subject.

 Read the sample encyclopedia entry below. Use it to answer the questions that follow.

> **WATER** is a liquid. Like air (oxygen), water is necessary for all living things. A person can live only a few days without water. Water is lost from the body every day and must be replaced. Drinking and eating replace water. About 60 percent of a person's body weight is water. *See also* OXYGEN.

1. What is the article about? _____

2. Why is water important? _____

3. How much of a person's body is water? _____

4. How is water in the body replaced? _____

5. What other subject could you look under to get more information? _____

6. What could be another related topic? _____

> **OXYGEN** is a gas that has no smell, no taste, and no color. Nearly all living things need oxygen to live. Oxygen mixes with other things in a person's body to produce energy needed for life processes. Oxygen is also an important part of water. Oxygen is sometimes called air.

7. How are oxygen and water the same? _____

8. Does the above cross-reference mention water? _____

9. How does the article describe oxygen? _____

10. What is another word for oxygen? _____

Unit 6: Study Skills
Language: Usage and Practice 5, SV 1419027824

Name _____   Date _____

Using an Encyclopedia, p. 2

When looking for an article in the encyclopedia:
- Look up the last name of a person.
  EXAMPLE: To find an article on Babe Ruth, look under <u>Ruth</u>.
- Look up the first word in the name of a city, state, or country.
  EXAMPLE: To find an article on New York City, look under <u>New</u>.
- Look up the most important word in the name of a general topic.
  EXAMPLE: To find an article on the brown bear, look under <u>bear</u>.

❋ **Write the word you would look under to find an article on each of the following subjects.**

11. Susan B. Anthony _____

12. salt water _____

13. New Mexico _____

14. lakes in Scotland _____

15. Rio de Janeiro _____

16. United Kingdom _____

17. modern literature _____

18. breeds of horses _____

❋ **The example below shows how the volumes of one encyclopedia are marked. The volumes are numbered. The subjects are in alphabetical order. Write the number of the volume in which you would find each article.**

A	B	C–CH	Cl–CZ	D	E	F	G	H	I–J	K
1	2	3	4	5	6	7	8	9	10	11

L	M	N	O	P	Q–R	S	T	U–V	W–Z
12	13	14	15	16	17	18	19	20	21

_____ 19. caring for chickens

_____ 20. the flag of the United States

_____ 21. how glass is made

_____ 22. vitamins

_____ 23. reptiles

_____ 24. the history of Japan

_____ 25. how rainbows are formed

_____ 26. pine trees

Unit 6: Study Skills
Language: Usage and Practice 5, SV 1419027824

Name _____   Date _____

Unit 6 Test

Darken the circle by the correct answer to each question.

1. Which of the following steps would come first?
   - Ⓐ Apply second coat of paint.
   - Ⓑ Scrape away old, flaky paint.
   - Ⓒ Apply paint with smooth, even strokes.
   - Ⓓ Stir paint well.

2. Which would you do after mixing all ingredients together?
   - Ⓐ Put in microwave-safe dish.
   - Ⓑ Stir well and put back in microwave for 10 minutes.
   - Ⓒ Set timer for 20 minutes.
   - Ⓓ Start microwave oven.

Which group of words is in alphabetical order? Darken the circle by the correct choice.

3. | Ⓐ pair | Ⓑ germ | Ⓒ quake | Ⓓ seal |
pear	gear	quest	search
part	gem	quiver	section
page	gelatin	quick	serve

4. | Ⓐ dog | Ⓑ back | Ⓒ scamp | Ⓓ pert |
doing	bacteria	scan	peeve
dwindle	bagful	scare	pester
dwell	bagel	scat	person

Which word would be on the same page as the guide words? Darken the circle by the correct choice.

5. card / case
   - Ⓐ capital
   - Ⓑ cabin
   - Ⓒ carrot
   - Ⓓ cast

6. vacate / vain
   - Ⓐ valentine
   - Ⓑ vacant
   - Ⓒ van
   - Ⓓ vacation

Which shows the correct division of the word into syllables? Darken the circle by the correct choice.

7. carefully
   - Ⓐ ca-re-fu-lly
   - Ⓑ care-ful-ly
   - Ⓒ care-full-y
   - Ⓓ care-fu-lly

8. forgotten
   - Ⓐ for-got-ten
   - Ⓑ for-gotten
   - Ⓒ for-go-tten
   - Ⓓ for-go-tt-en

9. skyscraper
   - Ⓐ sk-yscra-per
   - Ⓑ sky-scra-per
   - Ⓒ sky-scrap-er
   - Ⓓ sky-scrape-r

10. beautiful
    - Ⓐ bea-u-ti-ful
    - Ⓑ beaut-i-ful
    - Ⓒ be-au-ti-ful
    - Ⓓ beau-ti-ful

Language: Usage and Practice 5, SV 1419027824

Name _____ Date _____

Darken the circle by the correct answer to each question.

11. Which is <u>not</u> part of an encyclopedia?

  Ⓐ guide words

  Ⓑ dictionary

  Ⓒ volumes

  Ⓓ subjects in alphabetical order

12. In which volume would the importance of the water cycle be found?

  Ⓐ C

  Ⓑ T

  Ⓒ W

  Ⓓ I

Use the sample encyclopedia article to answer the questions.
Darken the circle by the correct choice.

> **BRAN** Bran is the outer layers of food grains. When flour is made, the outer layers of grain come off. These particles are bran. Bran is a very healthful food. It is full of vitamins and minerals. Bran is used as a breakfast food and as an ingredient in baking. Pure bran is dark brown in color. Pure bran is often combined with other cereal grains, such as wheat. *See also* FIBER and CEREAL.

13. What is the article about?

  Ⓐ flour

  Ⓑ grains

  Ⓒ vitamins

  Ⓓ bran

14. What is bran?

  Ⓐ outer particles of grain

  Ⓑ flour

  Ⓒ wheat

  Ⓓ a color

15. How is bran obtained?

  Ⓐ by taking off the outer layers of grains

  Ⓑ by baking grains

  Ⓒ by combining grains

  Ⓓ by coloring grains

16. What are the cross-references?

  Ⓐ flour and grain

  Ⓑ fiber and cereal

  Ⓒ vitamins and minerals

  Ⓓ cereal and wheat

Darken the circle by the volume in an encyclopedia where each article would be found.

A–C	D–F	G–I	J–L	M–N	O–Q	R–S	T–V	W–Z
1	2	3	4	5	6	7	8	9

17. the city of Springfield

  Ⓐ I   Ⓒ 7

  Ⓑ 6   Ⓓ 8

18. Walt Disney

  Ⓐ 1   Ⓒ 8

  Ⓑ 2   Ⓓ 9

Language Terms

abbreviation   a short form of a word

action verb   a verb that tells an action that the subject is doing

adjective   a word that describes a noun by telling which one, what kind, or how many

adverb   a word that describes a verb, adjective, or another adverb

antonym   a word that has the opposite meaning of another word

apostrophe   a mark used to show where the missing letter or letters would be in a contraction; an apostrophe is also used in possessive nouns

common noun   a noun that does not name a particular person, place, or thing

compound sentence   two simple sentences joined together by words such as and, but, so, and or

compound word   a word formed by putting two or more words together

conjunction   a word that joins words or groups of words

contraction   a word formed by joining two other words and leaving out some letters

declarative sentence   a sentence that makes a statement

exclamatory sentence   a sentence that shows surprise or emotion

helping verb   a word used to help the main verb of the sentence, usually a form of the verb to be

homonym   a word that sounds like another word but has a different meaning and is spelled differently

imperative sentence   a sentence that gives a command

interjection   a word or group of words that expresses strong feeling

interrogative sentence   a sentence that asks a question

linking verb   a verb that does not show action but links the subject to a word that either describes the subject or gives the subject another name

noun   a word that names a person, place, or thing

object pronoun   a pronoun used after an action verb or after words such as to, with, for, and by

paragraph   a group of sentences about one main idea

plural noun   a noun that names more than one person, place, or thing

possessive noun   a noun that tells who or what owns something

possessive pronoun   a pronoun that tells who or what owns something

predicate   the part of a sentence that tells what the subject does or what happens to the subject

prefix   a syllable added to the beginning of a word to change the meaning of the word

preposition   a word that shows the relationship of a noun or pronoun to another word in the sentence

prepositional phrase   a group of words that begins with a preposition and ends with a noun or pronoun

pronoun   a word that takes the place of a noun

proper noun   a noun that names a particular person, place, or thing and is capitalized

proper adjective   an adjective formed from a proper noun; a proper adjective is capitalized

quotation   the exact words a person said

run-on sentence   two or more sentences that run together without correct punctuation

sentence   a group of words that expresses a complete thought

simple predicate   the main word or words in the predicate part of a sentence

simple sentence   a sentence that has one subject and one predicate

simple subject   the main word in the subject part of a sentence

singular noun   a noun that names one person, place, or thing

subject   the part of a sentence that tells who or what the sentence is about

suffix   a syllable added to the end of a word to change the meaning of the word

synonym   a word that has the same or almost the same meaning as another word

topic sentence   a sentence that tells the main idea of a paragraph

verb   the main word in the predicate

verb tense   the time expressed by the verb

Answer Key

Assessment
Pages 7–10
1. S
2. H
3. A
4. H
5. ball
6. C
7. P
8. S
9. C
10. will not
11. he will
The words in bold should be circled.
12. E, **days**, are
13. IN, **you**, do mean
14. D, **I**, like
15. IM, **You**, should take
16. CS
17. CP
18. RO
19. CS
20. Underline: dog, park. Circle: Jon, Rachel
21. car's
22. H
23. L
24. A
25. future
26. past
27. present
28. Did, see
29. drank, broke
30. written, sung
31. ate, began
32. PP
33. SP
34. OP
35. adjective
36. adverb
37. The words in bold should be circled.
on the floor
of the garage.
38. Teach
39. good
40. set
41. sit
42. may

Letter: 487 E. Deer Run
Sacramento, CA 94099
Feb. 27, 2007

Dear Luke,
What's it like living in California? I can't even imagine it. The postcards you sent were fantastic! It will be fun to come and visit. I'm worried about earthquakes, though.
Take care of yourself.
Your friend,
Paul
43.–46. Answers will vary.
47. 3
48. 1
49. 2
50. slum-ber
51. smat-ter-ing
52. slug-gish
53. locks
54. help ships move through canals
55. two
56. stairs
57. canal
58. 5, mining
59. 7, Twain
60. 5, Nile
61. 7, tundra
62. 7, Sweden
63. 3, Great
64. 3, gardens
65. 8, volcanoes

Unit 1
Page 11
Answers will vary. Check that synonyms are used as directed.

Page 12
Answers will vary. Suggested antonyms:
1. light
2. lazy
3. down
4. quiet
5. south
6. sell
7. night
8. sweet
9. go
10. bad
11. large
12. smooth
13. white
14. below
15. smiling
16. over
17. ugly
18. hot
19. weak
20. narrow
21. happy
22. west
23. warm
24. start
25. light
26. short
27. take
28. easy
29.–38. Antonyms will vary.

Page 13
1.–6. Phrase content will vary.
Suggested homonyms:
1. hall
2. rode
3. some
4. weigh
5. knew
6. meet
7. too, to
8. two
9. to, two, too
10. to, two, to
11. there, their
12. They're, their
13. They're, their

Page 14
1. to
2. well
3. It's
4. your
5. Two, there
6. its
7. You're
8. too
9. good
10. They're
11. well
12. their
13. it's
14. two
15. They're
16. two, there

Page 15
1. b
2. b
3. a
4. b
5. b
6. snap
7. limp
8. row
9. bark
10. squash
11.–12. Sentences will vary.

Page 16
1. kindness, the state of being kind
2. predate, to date before
3. helpless, without help
4. remade, made again
5. relives
6. endless
7. darkness
8. predawn
9. misread
10. delightful

Page 17
1. who's
2. couldn't
3. they've
4. I'll
5. doesn't
6. should've
7. you'd
8. I've
9. that's
10. didn't
11. let's
12. they're
13. wasn't
14. Where's
15. She's
16. I've
17. can't
18. What'll
19. Let's
20. he'll
21. What's
22. it's
23. I'm or it's
24. couldn't

Page 18
1. high/way
2. old/time
3. full/moon
4. snow/flake
5. air/conditioner
6. fire/drill
7. bare/foot

Language: Usage and Practice 5, SV 1419027824

8. baby/sitter
9. splash/down
10. sweat/shirt
11. high/rise
12. earth/quake
13. half/mast
14. bull/dog
15. skate/board
16. hardware or neighborhood
17. backyard or neighborhood
18. afternoon
19. outcome
20. neighborhood
21. houseboat, boathouse
22. cupcake, cakewalk

Page 19
1. will
2. a
3. are
4. anything
5. anybody
6. ever
7. any
8. There are no more than four kinds of poisonous snakes in North America.
9. It won't do any good to try to run away from a rattlesnake.
10. Don't ever tease a snake that might bite you.

Page 20
Sentences will vary.
1. Our family was packing suitcases.
2. Everyone was looking forward to our annual vacation.
3. When all the suitcases were packed, Mom loaded the trunk.
4. We left at noon on Saturday.
5. We drove to the freeway.
6. We stopped often because my little brother was ill.
7. The first day of travel seemed fine, though.
8. The second day we visited historical places.
9. Everyone enjoyed the rest of the trip, too.
10. Everyone welcomed us back.

Page 21
Senses may vary.
1. blue, sight
2. cool, touch
3. large, sight
4. loud, hearing
5. chlorine, smell
6. jagged, touch or sight
7. rough, touch
8. soft, touch
9. warm, touch
10. delicious, taste

Page 22
1. wonderful
2. Brave
3. fascinating
4. hilarious
5. smile
6. cheap
7. soggy
8. nagged
9. stubborn
10. silly
11. A disaster is more serious than a problem.
12. An antique is worth more than something old.

Page 23
Answers will vary. Possible responses are given.
1. I was very nervous.
2. As I looked out over the audience, I had a heavy feeling in my chest.
3. I touched the piano keys, and my fingers were stiff.
4. Luckily for me, the performance went very well.
5. As I played the last notes, I knew that I had done well.
6.–7. Responses will vary.

Unit 1 Test
Pages 24–25
1. C	11. C	21. D
2. A	12. B	22. A
3. B	13. D	23. C
4. C	14. C	24. B
5. D	15. D	25. C
6. B	16. D	26. C
7. D	17. C	27. B
8. A	18. A	28. D
9. B	19. D	29. A
10. C	20. C	30. B

Unit 2
Page 26
1.–10. Sentences will vary. Be sure each sentence contains a subject or predicate as needed.

Page 27
S should precede the following sentences:
3, 6, 7, 9, 10, 12, 13, 15, 17
Sentences will vary.

Page 28
1. interrogative
2. declarative
3. interrogative
4. declarative
5. declarative
6. interrogative
7. interrogative
8. declarative
9.–16. Sentences and labels will vary.

Page 29
1. imperative
2. exclamatory
3. imperative
4. imperative
5. exclamatory
6. imperative
7. exclamatory
8. exclamatory
9. imperative
10. imperative
11. exclamatory
12. imperative
13. imperative
14. exclamatory
Sentences will vary.

Page 30
1. S
2. P
3. P
4. S
5. S
6. P
7.–17. Subjects and predicates will vary.

Page 31
Students should circle the words in bold.
1. Freshly-picked **morels** / are . . .
2. These **mushrooms** / can . . .
3. A rich **soil** / is . . .
4. Grassy **spots** / are . . .
5. The **spring** / must . . .
6. Damp **earth** / is . . .
7. A clear, sunny **sky** / means . . .
8. **We** / never . . .
9. Tall, wet **grasses** / often . . .
10. **We** / must . . .
11. These spongy little **mushrooms** / do . . .
12. **You** / might . . .
13.–17. Sentences will vary.

Page 32
Students should circle the words in bold.
1. Many tourists / **visit** the Netherlands in April or May.
2. The beautiful tulip blooms / **reach** their height of glory during these months.
3. Visitors / **can see** flowers for miles and miles.
4. Jan / **is dreaming** of a trip to the Netherlands someday.
5. She / **has seen** colorful pictures of tulips in catalogs.
6. The catalogs / **show** tulips of all colors in full bloom.

7. Jan / **is** anxious to see the tulips herself.
8. Passing travelers / **can** buy large bunches of flowers.
9. Every Dutch city / **has** flowers everywhere.
10. Flower vases / **can be found** in the cars of some Dutch people.
11.–13. Predicates will vary.
14.–17. Sentences will vary.

Page 33
1. (You) Turn
2. (You) turn
3. (You) Park
4. (You) Do block
5. (You) Leave
6. (You) Help
7. (You) Hold
8. (You) Get
9. (You) Lock
10. (You) Check
11. (You) Knock
12. (You) Try
13.–16. Sentences will vary.

Page 34
1. C, Paul Bunyan and Babe
2. Babe
3. C, Maine and Minnesota
4. Babe
5. C, Lumberjacks and storytellers
6. Tennessee and Texas claim Davy Crockett as their hero.
7. Great bravery and unusual skills made Davy Crockett famous.
8. True stories and tall tales about Davy Crockett were passed down.
9. These true stories and tall tales made Davy Crockett a legend.
10. Sentences will vary.

Page 35
1. C, wrote and printed its own newspaper.
2. was named editor-in-chief.
3. C, assigned the stories and approved the final copies.
4. were reporters.
5. C, wrote the news stories or edited the stories.
6. C, interviewed a new student and wrote the interview.
Sentences may vary. Suggested:
7. Casey covered the baseball game and described the best plays.
8. Allison and Kim wrote jokes and made up puzzles.
9. Luis corrected the news stories and wrote headlines.
10. Alex typed the newspaper but couldn't print it.
11. Sentences will vary.

Page 36
1. S, George Washington / witnessed
2. C, John Adams / was; his son / was
3. S, Thomas Jefferson / was
4. C, The British / burned; President Madison / escaped
Sentences may vary. Suggested:
5. Andrew Jackson was called "Old Hickory," and Zachary Taylor's nickname was "Old Rough and Ready."
6. Four presidents had no children, but John Tyler had fourteen children.
7. Chester A. Arthur put the first bathroom in the White House, and Benjamin Harrison put in electric lights.
8. Woodrow Wilson coached college football, and Ronald Reagan announced baseball games on radio.

Page 37
Answers may vary. Possible response:
Each year, King Minus demanded a human sacrifice from the people of Athens. Seven boys and seven girls would enter the Labyrinth. The Labyrinth was the home of the Minotaur. The Minotaur was half man and half beast. The boys and girls were devoured by the Minotaur. Finally, Theseus found and killed the Minotaur in the Labyrinth.

Page 38
1. Lashonda waited patiently and quietly.; adverbs
2. She had felt disappointed and rejected before.; adjectives
3. She really and truly wanted to be a scientist.; adverbs
4. Lashonda read the letter slowly and calmly.; adverbs
5. She was happy and excited about the news; adjectives
6. She spread the news happily and quickly.; adverbs
7. Her parents were proud and excited.; adjectives
8. Lashonda began to pack quickly and carefully.; adverbs

Page 39
1. Patrick studied the wall, and he found a hidden button.
2. Patrick pushed the button, and the bookcase moved.
3. Patrick could wait, or he could explore the path.
4. He wasn't afraid, but he wasn't comfortable, either.

5. Patrick thought about what to do, and he decided to explore.
6. The path was dark, and Patrick felt nervous.
7. He started down the path, but he stopped when he heard a noise.

Page 40
1. The sunlight shone on the little door.
2. Into the shack walked Angela and Jacob.
3. A large wooden table was inside the shack.
4. A black cat lay on the table.
5. Cannot be changed; inverting would change meaning.
6. A witch's magic was at work in the shack!
7. Cannot be changed; inverting would change meaning.
8. The two friends went out the door.

Page 41
Corrections of sentences may vary.
1. A box turtle is a reptile. It lives in woods and fields.
2. Simple sentence
3. It can pull its legs, head, and tail inside its shell and get "boxed in."
4. Many kinds of turtles live on land and in the water.
5. Turtles belong to the same family as lizards, snakes. alligators, and crocodiles.
6. Simple sentence
7. Painted turtles eat meal worms, earthworms, minnows, and insects. The musk turtle finds food along the bottoms of ponds or streams.
8. Painted turtles get their name from the red and yellow patterns on their shells. They also have yellow lines on their heads.

Page 42
1. There are over two hundred kinds of marsupials. All live in North or South America or in Australia.
2. The kangaroo is the largest marsupial. The male red kangaroo may be up to seven feet tall.
3. Wallabies are similar to kangaroos. They are smaller than kangaroos. Some are the size of a rabbit.
4. Kangaroos and wallabies live only in Australia. Their hind feet are larger than their front feet.
Paragraph:
Opossums are the only marsupials that live north of Mexico. They also live in Central and South America. Opossums are grayish white. They

have a long snout, hairless ears, and a long, hairless tail. Opossums have fifty teeth. The opossum mother has from five to twenty babies. Each baby is the size of a kidney bean.

Unit 2 Test
Pages 43–44

1. B	7. D	13. A
2. D	8. C	14. B
3. B	9. B	15. C
4. A	10. A	16. C
5. C	11. A	17. B
6. D	12. D	18. A

Unit 3
Page 45

1.–5. Nouns will vary.
6. section, United States, scenes, beauty
7. trees, California, giants, forest
8. fall, tourists, trees, Vermont
9. cities, beaches
10. flowers, grasses, prairies, Texas
11. Montana, Wyoming, mountains
12. citizens, state, pride, charm, state

Page 46

1.–18. Proper nouns will vary.
19.–36. Common nouns will vary.

Page 47

1. P, boot	12. P, sky
2. S, armies	13. S, wives
3. S, matches	14. P, box
4. P, map	15. S, beaches
5. P, inch	16. S, books
6. S, feet	17. stories
7. S, heroes	18. watches
8. S, alleys	19. players
9. S, babies	20. shelves
10. P, woman	21. monkeys
11. P, half	22. children

Page 48

1. trout	8. wolves
2. fish or fishes	9. oxen
3. heroes	10. calves
4. women	11. geese
5. men	12. children
6. mice	13. feet
7. beliefs	14. lives

Page 49

1. dog's	12. cat's
2. neighbor's	13. dinosaur's
3. plane's	14. team's
4. Ann's	15. Amanda's friend
5. grandmother's	
6. tiger's	16. the friend's car
7. sister's	17. the play's director
8. brother's	
9. mother's	18. the lion's roar
10. truck's	19. the tiger's growl
11. teacher's	

Page 50

1. horses, horse's, horses'
2. birds, bird's, birds'
3. teachers, teacher's, teachers'
4. children, child's, children's
5. trucks, truck's, trucks'
6. doctors, doctor's, doctors'
7. men, man's, men's
8. churches, church's, churches'
9. The Smiths' cat has three kittens.
10. The kittens' names are Frisky, Midnight, and Puff.
11. The neighbors' dogs are very playful.
12. The dogs' pen is in the yard.
13. The cats' curiosity might get them into trouble.

Page 51

1. started	Verbs may vary.
2. recycle	Suggested:
3. buy	13. worried
4. recycled	14. studied
5. threw	15. hoped, knew, felt, thought
6. burned	
7. harmed	16. thought
8. asked	17. remember
9. recycle	18. felt
10. throw	19. hoped, knew, thought, felt
11. work	
12. recycle	20. believe

Page 52

1. linking: felt
2. action: left
3. action: needed
4. action: looked
5. action: saw
6. action: ran; studied
7. linking: appeared
8. action: pulled; moved
9. action: slid
10. action: hurried
11. action: bowed
12. linking: was
13. linking: was
14. linking: was

Page 53

Students should circle the words in bold.

1. **Have** heard
2. **was** born
3. **could** make
4. **were** telling
5. was (no helping verb)
6. **had** climbed
7. **was** carrying
8. **had been** pouring
9. **was** covered
10. **were** running
11. **could** make
12. saw (no helping verb)
13. jumped (no helping verb)

14. did (no helping verb)
15. sing (no helping verb)
16. would
17. have
18. will
19. will
20. would

Page 54

1. tells	9. had reached
2. plays	10. trailed
3. makes	11. were called
4. call	12. left, went
5. is	13. made
6. frightens	14. came
7. hits	15. went
8. love	16. struck

17.–20. Verbs will vary.

Page 55

1. done	8. said
2. rode	9. took
3. gave	10. thought
4. ran	11. written
5. come	12. went
6. ate	13. gave
7. saw	14. did

Page 56

1. began	9. found
2. grew	10. torn
3. known	11. rang
4. chosen	12. caught
5. spoken	13. swum
6. flew	14. brought
7. worn	15. sang
8. lost	

Page 57

Verbs will vary. Suggested:

1. will write, will send	10. will receive
	11. will mail
2. will decide	12. will study
3. will fill	13. will choose
4. will make	14. will plan
5. will bake	15. will write
6. will think	16. will design
7. will hide	17. will make
8. will shout	18. will hope
9. will send	

Page 58

1. P / stories, tell
2. S / story, says
3. S / Wild Dog, becomes
4. P / dogs, leave
5. S / dog, doesn't
6. P / people, don't
7. P / Diggings, prove
8. P / Bones, do
9. P / vases, picture
10. S / organization, trains
11. P / eyes, have
12. S / dog, does
13. S / person, doesn't
14. P / Dogs, are
15. S / dog, brings

Page 59
1. S / Tracy, is
2. P / brothers, are
3. P / Tracy and her brothers, were
4. S / Tracy, was
5. P / brothers, were
6. P / people, were
7. S / Tracy, was
8. P / brothers, were
9. S or P / you, were
10. S / Tracy, is
11. is
12. Isn't
13. is
14. was
15. was
16. were
17. are
18. was
19. is
20. are

Page 60
1. did
2. gone
3. sang
4. sung, did
5. seen
6. sung
7. sang
8. went
9. done
10. saw
11. seen
12. did
13. gone
14. sung
15. gone
16. went
17. saw
18. gone
19. done
20. seen
21. sang

Page 61
1. took
2. taken
3. wrote
4. drank
5. taken
6. broke
7. wrote
8. written
9. drunk
10. taken
11. taken
12. drunk
13. broken
14. broken
15. written

Page 62
1. gave
2. eaten
3. ate
4. given
5. eaten
6. gave
7. rang
8. drawn
9. drew
10. rung
11. eaten
12. rung
13. eaten
14. given
15. drawn
16. given
17. drew

Page 63
1. begun
2. thrown
3. began
4. fallen
5. threw
6. fell
7. fallen
8. stolen
9. stole
10. begun
11. fell
12. threw
13. thrown
14. thrown
15. stolen
16. begun
17. thrown
18. begun

Page 64
1. Statue of Liberty
2. pieces
3. crates
4. statue
5. immigrants
6. statue
7. torch
8. hope, freedom
9.–18. Sentences will vary. Be sure each sentence contains an appropriate direct object.

Page 65
1. They, Explorers
2. It, animal
3. them, animals or kangaroos
4. They, birds
5. It, platypus
6. They, Scientists
7. It, coolabah or tree
8. It, flower or kangaroo paw

Page 66
1. He, Mr. Les Harsten
2. them, plants
3. He, Les
4. It, sound
5. He, Les
6. it, plant
7. them, sounds
8. It, recording
9. They, plants
10. It, music
11. They, plants
12. they, sounds

Page 67
1. She
2. He
3. They
4. She
5. It
6. She
7. she
8. She
9. me
10. us
11. him
12. them
13. us
14. them
15. us

Page 68
1. her
2. hers
3. our
4. hers, mine
5. our
6. ours
7. my, hers
8. yours
9. Your
10. Its
11. Its
12. his
13. his
14. My
15. our

Page 69
1. myself
2. himself
3. itself
4. herself
5. yourselves
6. ourselves
7. yourself
8. themselves
9. ourselves
10. herself
11. myself
12. herself
13. himself
14. themselves

Page 70
1. early, healthy, important; Greeks, body
2. strong, healthy; bodies, minds
3. distant; past
4. great, powerful; god, Cronus
5. high, beautiful; peaks, mountains
6. mighty, first, peaceful; struggle, Olympics, valley
7.–16. Adjectives will vary.

Page 71
1. Greek, Greece
2. Spartan, Sparta
3. Athenian, Athens
4. Roman, Rome
5. Korean, Korea
6. Romanian, Romania
7. English
8. Norwegian
9. Canadian
10. American
11. Russian
12. Japanese

Page 72
1. crunchy; peanuts
2. salty; They
3. red; skin
4. delicious; seeds
5. inedible; seeds
6. popular; They
7. healthful; snacks
8. sour; apples
9. crisp and juicy; fruit
10. noisy; vegetable
11.–15. Adjectives will vary.

Page 73
1. a
2. These
3. the
4. this
5. a
6. the
7. a
8. this
9. the
10. these
11. A, the
12. those

Page 74
1. biggest
2. largest
3. more interesting
4. larger
5. more accurate
6. higher
7. biggest
8. most popular
9. prettiest
10. greatest
11. finest
12. hardest
13. best
14. better
15. most amazing

Page 75
1. better
2. less
3. worst
4. more
5. worse
6. more
7. Many
8. most

Page 76
1. talked; daily; how often
2. walked; often; how often

www.harcourtschoolsupply.com
© Harcourt Achieve Inc. All rights reserved.

Answer Key
Language: Usage and Practice 5, SV 1419027824

3. had; seldom; how often
4. decided; suddenly; when
5. slipped; quietly; how
6. crept; carefully; how
7. opened; quietly; how
8. peered; then; when
9. swept; instantly; when
10. banged; loudly; how
11. ran; swiftly; how
12. returned; never; how often
13. late
14. nervously
15. Suddenly
16. finally

Page 77
1. closer
2. earlier
3. faster
4. more quickly
5. more patiently
6. more carefully
7. more quietly
8. sooner
9. most skillfully
10. more happily
11. biggest
12. deeper
13. bravest
14. stronger

Page 78
1. very
2. extremely
3. carefully
4. quite
5. too
6. fairly
7. certainly
8. rather
9. much
10. charming
11. suggests
12. uses
13. work
14. decided
15. less
16. beautiful
17. proud
18. difficult
19. complicated
20. long

Page 79
Adverbs are indicated in bold print.
1. Three, rugged; **once**
2. wild; **finally, there**
3. different; **usually**
4. zoo, three, bear
5. young, comfortable, new, distant; **soon**
6. hilly, hopeful, six; **quietly, then, down**
7. next, rocky, powerful; **carefully**
8. huge, brown, three; **playfully**
9. two, that; **quietly**
10. large; **barely**
11. wise; **never, uphill**
12. human, watchful, mother; **immediately**
13. fierce, beady; **heavily, out, up**
14. red, dirty; **tightly**
15. curious; **clumsily**
16. wide; **Quickly, below**

17. clever; **successfully**
18. many; **finally**

Page 80
These phrases should be underlined, and students should circle the words in bold.
1. **on** the dining room table
2. **of** Marta's
3. **for** weeks
4. **in** her bedroom
5. **into** the dining room
6. **to** the floor
7. **to** the dining room
8. **under** the table
9. **on** her face

Paragraph:
When I went into the store, I looked at coats. I needed a new one to wear during the winter. I left my old one on the bus. When I got on the bus, I noticed it was very hot. I removed my coat and put it under my seat. When I got off the bus, I forgot it. When I asked about it, I was told to look at the office. It was not in the office.

Directions:
Answers will vary.

Page 81
Words in bold should be circled.
1. **in** a car
2. **from** the sea
3. **from** the motion; **of** the waves
4. **In** this same way; **in** the back; **of** a car
5. **of** balance
6. **inside** your ears
7. **with** a fluid; **with** special hairs
8. **of** movement
9. **in** the bottom; **of** the canals
10. **around** the canals
11. **in** your stomach
12.–14. Sentences will vary. Be sure that each sentence contains a prepositional phrase.

Page 82
1. and
2. but
3. and
4. or
5. but
6. or
7. and
8. and
9. or
10. and
11. and
12. but

Page 83
1. Gee!
2. Wow!
3. Oh, dear!
4. Oh, my!
5. Good grief!
6. Oops!
7. Great!
8. Alas!
9. Of course!
10. Gosh!
11.–20. Sentences will vary. Be sure that each sentence contains an interjection.

Page 84
1. May
2. may, can
3. well
4. good
5. May
6. can
7. well
8. good
9. may
10. may
11. can
12. can
13. can, well
14. good
15. well
16. good
17. well
18. good
19. can
20. well

Page 85
1. teach
2. learn
3. teach
4. teach
5. learn
6. sit
7. set, sit
8. sit
9. teach
10. teach
11. sit
12. sit
13. teach
14. learn, set
15. Sit
16. set
17. sit
18. teach, set
19. set
20. sit

Unit 3 Test
Pages 86–87
1. C
2. D
3. B
4. A
5. D
6. C
7. A
8. B
9. A
10. B
11. A
12. B
13. C
14. C
15. A
16. D
17. B
18. A
19. D
20. B
21. C
22. B
23. C
24. B
25. A
26. C

Unit 4
Page 88
Students should circle the first letter of each sentence and then capitalize the following:
1. Have
2. Yung; Yes
3. So
4. He
5. I
6. We're

Students should circle the first letter of each sentence and then capitalize the following:
7. There, Lived, And, She
8. If, And, What, And
9. The, Song, Hiawatha
10. Down, River
11. *Up, Up, Away*
12. A Balloon Ride

Page 89
Students should circle the first letter of and then capitalize the following:
1. Larry
2. Chipper
3. Japanese, Tokyo, Japan
4. Scottish, Scotland
5. Larry, London
6. Sherlock Holmes

7. African, Mali, West Africa
8. Larry, Italian
9. Chipper's, Thailand
10.–14. Sentences will vary.

Page 90
Students should circle the first letter of and then capitalize the following:
1. Governor Potter, Senator Williams
2. Dr. Laura Bedford, Mayor Phillips
3. Rev. Barton, Mr. James Adams, Jr.
4. Prince Charles
5. Gen. David E. Morgan
   6656 N. Second Ave.
   Evanston, IL 60202
6. Valentine's Day Exhibit
   at Oak Grove Library
   Mon.-Fri., Feb. 10-14
   101 E. Madison St.
7. Sgt. Carlos M. Martinez
   17 Watling St.
   Shropshire SY7 OLW, England
4. Maxwell School Field Day
   Wed., Apr. 30, 1:00
   Register Mon.-Tues., Apr. 28-29
   Mr. Modica's office

Pages 91–92
1. .
2. .
3. ?
4. .
5. .
6. ?
7. ?
8. .
9. .

Paragraphs:

Have you ever wondered what it would be like to live as our country's pioneers did? You can visit log homes made to look like the original cabins of pioneer days. Then you can see how difficult life was for the pioneers who helped our country grow.

The cabins were small and roughly built. Many cabins had just one room. Where was the kitchen? Most of the cooking was done in the large fireplace. The fireplace also supplied the only heat. Wasn't it cold? You can be sure the winter winds whistled between the logs. And where did the pioneers sleep? Most cabins had a ladder reaching up to the bedroom loft.

The furniture in the cabins was usually as roughly built as the cabins themselves. All the clothing was handmade by the family. They ate food grown and caught on their land. Would you have liked to live in those times?

10. .
11. ?
12. .
13. .
14. !
15. .
16. .
17. ?
18. .
19. .
20. !; ?
21. .

Paragraphs:

Have you ever seen pictures of northern Minnesota? It is a region of many lakes. My family once spent a week on Little Birch Lake. What a sight it was!

There were thousands of white birches reflected in the blue water. The fishing was great! Every day we caught large numbers of bass, and every night we cooked fresh fish for our dinner.

The nearest town was Hackensack. At the waterfront was a large statue of Diana Marie Kensack. She is seated at the water's edge. Her gaze is fixed on the horizon. Do you know who she was? Legends say that she was Paul Bunyan's sweetheart. She is still waiting at the shore for him to come back to her. Be sure to visit Diana when you are in Minnesota!

Page 93
1. "Have you heard of the Nobel Peace Prize?" asked Emi.
2. "Yes. Mother Teresa and Nelson Mandela have won it," replied Jordan.
3. "But do you know who Nobel was?" Emi asked.
4. Jordan responded, "No, I guess I don't."
5. "He invented dynamite," stated Emi.
6. "It seems weird," said Jordan, "to name a peace prize for the inventor of dynamite."
7. "In fact," Emi said, "dynamite was once called Nobel's Safety Blasting Powder."
8. "Nobel patented the blasting powder in 1867," Emi continued.
9. "He did not want dynamite used for war," he said.
10. He added, "Nobel once said that war is the horror of horrors and the greatest of all crimes."
11. "How did the Nobel Prizes get started?" asked Jordan.
12. Emi said, "In his will, Nobel said that his money should be used to establish prizes in five areas: physics, chemistry, medicine, literature, and peace."
13. "Sometimes a prize is shared by two or three people," he continued.
14. "I'd like to know more about some of the winners," Jordan said.
15. "Jimmy Carter, 39th President of the United States, won the Nobel Peace prize in 2002," replied Emi.

Page 94
Apostrophe placement:
1. Chen's
2. children's
3. boys'
4. can't
5. Won't
6. people's
7. person's
8. Can't
9. don't, something's
10. what's

Colon placement:
11. 3:30
12. 6:00
13. 7:15
14. Dear Ms. Parson:

Pages 95–96
1. Cedarville, Taylorville, Gardner,
2. bridges, roads,
3. basement,
4. bailing, mopping,
5. blocks,
6. shrubs, flowers,
7. away,
8. lucky,
9. asked,
10. side,
11. joke,
12. asked,
13. asked,
14. beams,
15. Melody and Tim,
16. Oh,
17. Marie,
18. Well,
19. Ted,
20. No,
21. Oh,
22. Well,
23. Well,
24. Carlos,
25. Yes,
26. Oh,
27. Well,
28. Carlos,
29. Well,
Conversations will vary.

Unit 4 Test
Pages 97–98
1. A
2. B
3. B
4. C
5. B
6. A
7. B
8. B
9. A
10. C
11. C
12. C
13. D
14. A
15. B
16. D
17. C
18. D
19. B
20. C
21. D
22. C
23. B
24. A
25. C
26. B

Unit 5
Page 99
Answers will vary.

Page 100
Possible responses:
   Main Idea: how optical illusions occur

Detail: brain compares images you see to images in memory
Detail: brain cannot choose between possible interpretations
Detail: bending of light creates mirages that fool eyes

Page 101
Answers will vary.

Page 102
Sentences 2, 3, 4, and 6 should be underlined.
7. facts
Remaining answers will vary.

Page 103
1. b
2. b
3.–7. Sentences will vary.

Page 104
Students should underline these locations
Below me; the ball field; Across the street from the ball field; along the street; on the ball field; away from the street
Remaining answers will vary.

Page 105
Answers will vary.

Page 106
Answers will vary.

Page 107
1. patient, kind, generous
2. Possible details follow:
   The store is a block away.
   The owners' names are Mr. and Mrs. Aggens.
   Mrs. Aggens gives large scoops of ice cream.
   She doesn't hurry the writer.
   The writer had a decision to make.
   The store smelled of coffee.
3. The paragraph lacks color and interest.
Paragraphs will vary.

Page 108
1. house: weathered, old, had never known a paintbrush, gray; gate: rickety, crooked, hung on only its top hinge
2. breeze: gentle; grass: tall; moved: rippled; sweet peas: sugary; looked: lovely, white, pastel pink, and lavender
Paragraphs will vary.

Page 109
During the history of Earth, there have been several ice ages. These were times when giant sheets of ice spread across many parts of Earth. People think that almost one third of the land was covered by these huge sheets of ice.

The last ice age froze so much ocean water that the level of the oceans dropped. Then lots of land appeared that usually lay underwater. When the temperature began to warm up, the ice sheets melted. The ocean levels rose again.

Unit 5 Test
Pages 110–111
1. C	7. A	13. D
2. C	8. D	14. C
3. B	9. B	15. B
4. C	10. D	16. B
5. C	11. A	
6. C	12. C	

Unit 6
Page 112
1. Peanut Butter Balls
2. cookie sheet, bowl, measuring cup, teaspoon, stirring spoon
3. $\frac{1}{2}$ cup
4. wheat germ and sunflower seeds
5. 350°
6. 15 minutes
7. every 5 minutes
8. one teaspoonful
9. 3 hours
10. sesame seeds

Page 113
1. m, o
2. t, u, v
3. 3, 4, 2, 1
4. 3, 4, 1, 2
5. 3, 4, 1, 2
6. 2, 1, 3, 4
7. 2, 3, 1
8. 3, 1, 2
9. Caskey, Louis J.
   Caskey, T.C.
   Lyndale, Paul
   Lyons, Cindy

Page 114
1. Students should check blink, blame, blossom, blast, blaze, blouse.
2. Students should check into, introduce, iron, inward, invent, irrigate, invite.
3. meanwhile, melody, mention
4. professor, program, propeller, protest
5. receive, recess, reckon, recognize
6. miss, mist, mite

Page 115
1. chem-i-cal	21. de-ter-mine
2. gas-o-line	22. mu-si-cian
3. de-cree	23. sal-a-ry
4. mar-vel-ous	24. chee-tah
5. dis-ap-pear	25. in-ter-rupt
6. chim-ney	26. den-tist
7. con-ti-nen-tal	27. rec-og-nize
8. mis-er-a-ble	28. ras-cal
9. gen-er-al-ly	29. in-no-cent
10. gla-cier	30. ed-u-cate
11. a-rith-me-tic	31. a-chieve-ment
12. ex-er-cise	32. dar-ling
13. hos-pi-tal	33. home-stead
14. prob-lem	34. cal-en-dar
15. win-dow	35. mis-sion-ar-y
16. lan-guage	36. fare-well
17. ag-ri-cul-ture	37. a-lu-mi-num
18. par-a-keet	38. bac-te-ri-a
19. be-gin-ning	39. pro-gram
20. sim-ple	40. ba-nan-a

Pages 116–117
1. water
2. a person can live only a few days without water; water is necessary for all living things
3. about 60 percent
4. by eating and drinking
5. oxygen
6. air; liquid
7. Living things need both to live.
8. yes
9. a gas that has no smell, no taste, and no color
10. air	19. 3
11. Anthony	20. 20
12. salt	21. 8
13. New	22. 20
14. Scotland	23. 17
15. Rio	24. 10
16. United	25. 17
17. literature	26. 19
18. horses	

Unit 6 Test
Pages 118–119
1. B	7. B	13. D
2. A	8. A	14. A
3. D	9. C	15. A
4. C	10. D	16. B
5. C	11. B	17. C
6. D	12. C	18. B

Language: Usage and Practice 5, SV 1419027824